Liberated Publishing

Presents:

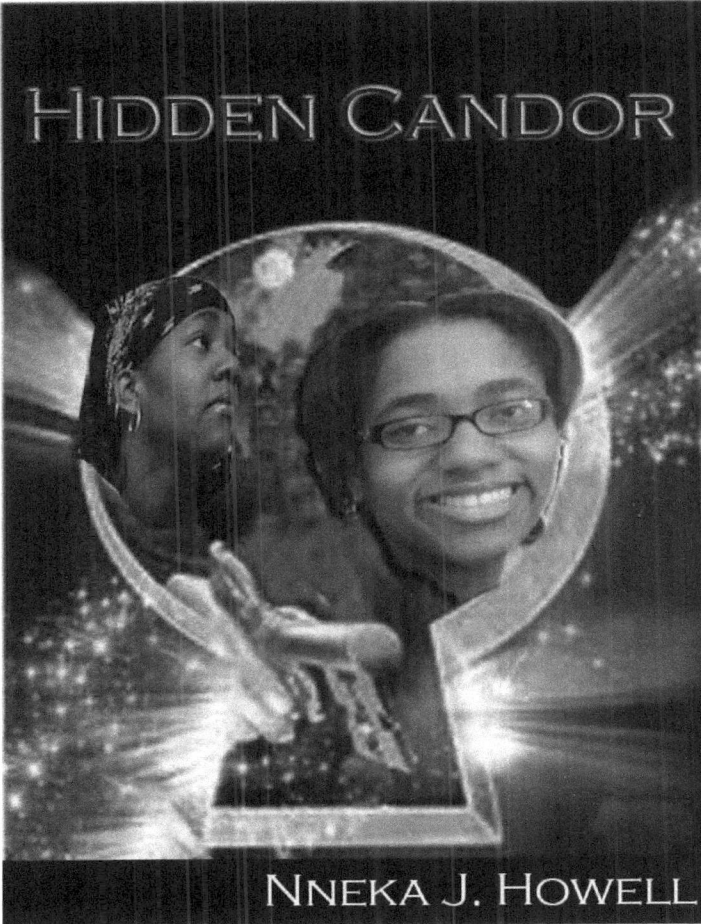

LiberatedPublishing.com

Liberated Publishing Inc.
1860 Wilma Rudolph Blvd
Clarksville, TN 37040

ISBN: 978-0-9825523-8-4

First Printing: July 2012

Printed in the United States of America

Hidden Candor:
Deciphered by Voice

HATE CURIOSITY
SUCCESS FAITH
DEFEAT RESPECT
LOVE LIES
POWER
JUSTICE PEACE

Book of Poetry

Written by: Nneka J. Howell

Special Thanks

God

Mother (Sandra J. Davis)

Grandmother (Willie M. Davis):
R.I.P

All of My Loved Ones, Family,
Friends, & Supporters!

Quotes to Live By

"He who does not understand your silence will probably not understand your words. "
- Elbert Hubbard

"Love smart, but NOT head first" – Nneka J. Howell
"If God be for me, who can be against me"
- *Romans 8:31*

"You can take the battles and the wars...I deserve the throne"
- Nneka J. Howell

"The first time someone shows you who they are, believe them."
- <u>Maya Angelou</u>

"Every thought in a possible action and every action is an opportunity. If you see it, you can grab it. If you lose it, you can find it. If you love it, you can care for it, and if you neglect it, you have chosen."
- Nneka J. Howell

"If I choose not to be a puppet of the norms, does that make me an ugly duck?"
- *Nneka J. Howell*

Contents

Intro: The I's of Poetry

Dosage 1: Dying to Live

Dosage 2: Outside In

Dosage 3: Just a View

Airplanes
Box Screen
Legally Black
Hand Gestures
My Skyline
God's Eye
Regardless of
Love Rush
Above Under
Karate Sex
Natural Vision
Just a View

Dosage 4: Competition with Self

Road rage
ONE MORE CHANCE
ZEBRA SKIN
BLACK RAIN
SIGN LANGUAGE
HAZARDS
A DAY AWAY
ZERO
I KNOW ME
TRANSFORMER
KIN FOLK
WORLD WAR III

Dosage 5: Lost In Perspective

Is It Love
Mistaken Identity
The Non-Existent Voice
Blue-N-Pink
Always
Symphony
Beneath the Pen
Blind Again
Head Lights
Quick Sand
Confirmed
Lady Love
Miss Me with That

Dosage 6: Wet-N-Dry

BUTTER BED
ON CALL
LESS THAN 60, MORE THAN 10
UNDER CONSTRUCTION
WISHFUL THINKING
ORIGAMI
FIRE HOES
LUSTFUL TRUST
DEEP DISH
LET'S GO FISHING
GYMNASTY
SPEAK YO BATTLE

Dosage 7: Justice Served

Tick-Toc
Even With Bars
Time = Lies
Black History
DUI
Verbal Phobia
Guilty
I Survived
The Best Revenge
Not Sorry
The Power of Green
Seduced

Dosage 8: Black & White

He Was Courteous
Death by Mic
Endless Love
Censored
Nickelodeon
A Dime for a Quarter
Simple
Before You
Sour Apple Face
Pizza Hut
A Dozen Puzzles
White
Kibbles & Bits
L.O.V.E

Dosage 9: A Step Ahead

Water Lilies
Reproduction
Spiral Staircases
Different Window View
Toy Story
A Mother's Spine
Book Bag
Corinthians
Love Notes Invisible
Stepping Out
Unreal Reality
Revulsion

Dosage 10: Forever Like Destiny

Just a Mattress
Fly To You
Animalistic
Cajun Love
Too Deep to Heal
Like Water
Concrete Flames
Open 24/7
Tiger Breath
Just Like Puberty
A Mother's Day
Destined by Quality

Dosage 11: Growth

He Saw the Best in Me
And There Was You
Centerpiece
Mountains Fall
Cubic Squares
Pencils, Erasers, & Paper
With One Touch
Size Matters
Taking Me Back
If It Were Me
Into Me

Dosage 12: Deciphered

Ameri-Kill
Fallen
White Rain
Damned Photo
Entitled
Hypocrisy
Life
Love Was, and Then
March On: A Grandmother's Wish
Regurgitate My Heart
Skeleton Go
So Much, So Little
From Purpose to Meaning
Amongst Us

Intro: The I's of Poetry

Throughout history, people have questioned the definition of poetry and its many components. Many think of it as a form of art that expands beyond just one perspective. In my opinion, poetry is an artistic way of expressing and challenging one's identity, desires, ability, and individuality. Words are more than just combined syllables. When a person has the power to intensify their words and birth a vivid meaning, it then has the ability to heal, burn, make, or take another's wounds. For me, poetry was a gift given way before I even knew how to read and write. While poetry may be a hobby for many, it is a lifestyle for me. Without poetry I no longer have an alternative world to go to when life is just too stressful. Being able to utilize such an art enables me to view the life around me from a unique lens.

There are five words that symbolize poetry in my eyes and they each start with the letter I. These five words are individualism, intensity, intimacy, irony, and identity. At some point and time, at least one of these words is consistent in every poem ever written, if not all of the words. Each word that a poem may contain breathes air that stimulates the reader's mind on different levels, depending on how much a person relates to the topic. When written passionately, poetry is an addiction for the reader and the author. However, there has been a debate on what poetry actually is and what it is not. In other words, can any form of writing be defined as poetry? This question alone has been a hot topic for decades. The truth is, any literature can be a symbol or definition of poetry. The fact that someone else may disagree with the structure or content of a written piece does not mean it isn't poetry. This form of art is diverse in many ways and perspectives in the sense that it is a very flexible way of writing.

For people like me, poetry is a virtue that serves as adrenaline in our bodies, rushing out of our minds like a bad habit. Some people utilize this art via spoken word, while others simply like to write it for private audiences or do both. I have been writing poetry since the fourth grade and has cherished it ever since. As author of poetry book *A Poet's Heart,* I have found many inspirations in the world of poetry. Not only do I look up to poets who came before me, such as June Jordan,

Maya Angelou, Gwendolyn Brooks, and Amiri Baraka, but I am also motivated by modern poets of today. Known as Lady Poet, I have worked hard to put my soul into my writing and I will continue to publish some of my best work so that others who come after me may see beauty beneath each stanza. I am poetry and poetry is I.

WELCOME TO THE REALMS OF POETRY!

Dosage 1: Dying to Live

Endangered Species: The Real Men Response

So I ask myself the same question -
where are all the real black men?
Says this woman inside of me
Illusionist or magician
Father figures keep disappearing
And to make it worse these men -
I mean these boys
keep making excuses for their wrong doings.

Let me paint the picture perfect
if only perfect paint existed
because this endangered species
is in need of a miracle.
I may sound cynical but
I speak of nothing but truth.
And love has become so secondary
that primary is distraction.
So distracted by the devil -
that love has become faint -
and so distracted by the devil
that intellect has become blank.

I am not saying that I'm such a saint
but I inhale and breathe ove.
I'm so loyal to being faithful -

that my pores bleed doves.
I mean my pores bleed peace
because that's all I hope to see -
when I look at the black man
who birthed me
and to think his rib is me?

Forget that, angry?
Yes I am.
Forgiving?
God said, so I will follow -
because if I stay angry at every ignorant black man
then I miss out on God's present upon my presence.
And not only to blame those black men who are so common,
It is also so rare to find a real woman.

Ladies degrade themselves just because
they feel they need to live up to HIS standards.
Girl wake the hell up,
Only God has the answers.
If a man can't love you for your intellectual beauty,
then why stoop to his level and just become his slave booty?

Why is it that we blame each other
for our own mistakes?
And why is it that love
is often converted into hate?
Black men wake up and realize
that some of us women are truthfully
QUEENS
And maybe if you weren't so stuck on
your fantasy dreams of sexing every girl
and thinking you're still SIXTEEN and
money over everything...

then you would realize a good thing when you got it...
oops I mean had it.
No need to play these childish games like
human beings are just some gadget.
You'll realize down the road...
that life only enables so many opportunities
and when you keep abusing them

God will pass that opportunity along to someone -
else who is grateful.
Someone who will suck the nectar of love
and enable -
the endangered species of men
to represent his origina creation.

IN BETWEEN

In between torn obstacles,
here lay shredded follicles
of turn tables that are overdosed
on heart aches so obvious.

Underneath each opportunity
I envision what you do to me
and after each melody
I see that I am thee felony.

You...
Make me insane
and turn me into this criminal.
I'm ready to scrape this off my teeth
like a dentist do...

Who...
told you that you had the right
to mislead me.
Who....
told you that my heart was funny?
Jokes, so greedy.

Needy me has been caught up
in needing this thing called love.
But the closer I get to caring,
the more I realize I must give up...

Because...
I know I cannot fight alone.
I'm weak, I'm blind...
God take me home...

And maybe I will...
breathe again.
Please take me from this world of sin.
I can't pretend like life isn't
a horrible hole to place me in...

In between torn obstacles,
here lay shredded follicles.
Suicide in the mirror...
No longer an option though....

Piece

Of

Mind

And if I were to peel back my scalp

And show you how cerebral I am

To allow my conclusions to run through you

Like a pulse after a track meet

And if I were to take my brain out

And place it in your palm

To allow your mind to wonder

How desperate would you become?

And if I were to get sick due to your own ignorance

Or my own

And fall over backwards

Just to give you back bone

And if I gave you all of this

And you have yet to wake up

Then it is time for me to walk away

Bottoms UP

$cholarship

Finances of the

        Majority?

                Debts of a believer

But the system is so

        Chopped up

           That definition leaves the sequel

Ideally who gets richer?

      And who gains more poverty?

                Who on top

And who shadows the beast?

     Tongue split with splinters soaked in blood

             Guilty by obsession

But not enough confession to share

       With the bear

               Who ate the lion

And the snail

      Who ate the snake!

              If we are equal

    HOW COME OUR MONEY AIN'T??!?!

@ My Best

I smoke like a factory chimney does
When it has been over worked and used
I like it when I imitate the idols on television
And wear nose bleed clothing just so my
Identity can portray the perfect image.
Oh and I love to worship those people
Who worship secret societies and
Put God last to everything
Life is beautiful when it's like this.
And how I love to drink heavy
Just so I can stay social or I do it
Cause my homies say what don't kill you-
Can't hurt you!
And I love having sex just because
I know I can get it.
With opportunities so easy-
I let my imagination run wild
Even if I'm the parent of this stupid unborn
CHILD.
And my perception is my own
I don't care who agrees and who
Doesn't
As far as I'm concerned I'm a dollar
To a dozen – pennies

And I love the adult I have become.

I still club hop, push guns, one night stand,

Steal, kill, drop out, and have a lot of fun.

What do you expect? I don't have a good role model

But society says I'm cool and humorous too (Who you think

they laughing at? Me or you?)

JUICES

Hawaiian punch is what they use in foreplay

It drizzles onto the tongue and masturbates your taste buds

I watch them as they swallow it, drip by drip

Left over moisture lay rested on pillow soft lips

But I know that it isn't as sweet as kool-aid

Biting my bottom lip I proceed mentally-

Thirsty for just a sample.

I fantasize about the entire encounter

Lipton, Welch's, Tropicana, Gatorade-

And the list goes on

So many things I can do with the shift of my tongue

And my eyes have deceived me, it was a must

I had to take what was theirs and desire for myself.

Five dollar bill attached to the counter top

Five for a dollar, such a great business exchange

What a super jag off, I had no control, nearly a fumble

It was hot as hell outside that particular day, so I just needed a drink!

You're Denial

I apologize in advance

for those who may accuse me of pre-judgment

but believe the experience, the truth is
more relevant

Harold camping is a false prophet —

A sharp tongue dipped in the depths of
hell.

How dare the people follow behind man,
without

Questioning him.

In the past, he was wrong, this time the
same thing

Judgment day will not proceed until **God**
writes it down-

in His planner.

The world is so undeserving of the mercy,

with all the hate and the worry,

I'm surprised the atmosphere hasn't
suffocated its inhabitants.

AND OSAMA BIN LADEN, YOU ALL CHEERED IN
AMAZING EXCITEMENT -

THIS IS WHAT YOU STAND FOR? *A DEAD MAN'S BODY?*

TWO HATE CRIMES DO NOT MAKE JUSTICE

AND IT DAMN SURE DOESN'T CREATE CHANGE.

PRESIDENTS CONFUSE ME; I'D RATHER LISTEN TO
THE BIBLE -

THAN TO VOTE AND PLEDGE ALLEGIANCE TO
HYPERCRITICAL IDOLS.

THIS POEM IS SUICIDAL, DUE TO YOUR DENIAL.

*DUE TO YOU'RE DENIAL, THE TRUTH IS
SUICIDAL.*

OLD SPICE

Tasteless

I enjoy the aroma of the beauty

Birds swim through the skies like time

Irreplaceable

Not even man-made machines can come close

To this elegance I am forever eager to see

Vibrant

In the night I watch the sun set like a perfect
legend

And it talks to me like my Father from heaven

Curious

It keeps me on my toes

The life of nature as it beams high on my life's
roads

Ambitious

It kicks in every time and never fails

And I embrace each moment, from the grass

To the sea shells

From the flowers to the pebbles

And the landscapes to the mysterious creations

I'm addicted to the ways of nature's good old
spice

Comma Incomplete

Neck-less

I choke

Like wingless doves

Beautiful but chosen last

Preference is always an eagle

No action verb exists with illiteracy

Can't read or speak my irreplaceable nature

Like a broken language, missing a grammatical banquet

And it was painless until I noticed the context

She took a deposit into the mirror with no receipt

It was tragic how the image was nothing like me

She wanted everything I had sacrificed and tried for

Didn't matter if it destroyed my torso's organ

Or if pain sucks away life's love

The mirror sheds like dog fur

I sneeze of bad allergies

She has left me

I am lost

Language error

Incomplete

Ugly Duck

I speak when not spoken to

I dislike pink as a female, I just tolerate
it

I'm not as weak as society portrays my sex

I don't prefer cats

And I'm proud I am Black

I hate the way you smoke weed and
cigarettes in my lungs

And I hate the way you drive with DUI's

You think it is cool to intercourse at a
young age

You think it is cool to homicide

You also think it is cool to follow the
crowd

And you follow trends because they do it on
TV

THE BEAUTIFUL IS UGLY

BUT I'D RATHER HAVE UGLY LIGHT THAN A
PRETTY MASK OF DARKNESS

I'D RATHER BE WITHOUT THAN WITH A LIE

I'D RATHER HAVE A CHOICE THAN TO BE TUGGED

I'D RATHER HAVE A TONGUE THAN SHOE TIED
LIPS

I'D RATHER DIE KNOWING THAT I AM AN
INDIVIDUAL

THAN TO LIVE AS A FLOCK

BUT I JUST HAVE ONE QUESTION

WOULD THAT MAKE ME AN UGLY DUCK?

Pizza & Pancakes

We are perpendicular

Us cannot be

You should love you

And I still have yet to love me

You love me because

You love the thought of me

I am a safe route to the

Uneasy rocky waters you side travel on

I love you but I can't

Give you me in pieces

I cannot allow myself to

Self destruct

Maybe we will never add up

Who said doubt was a bad thing?

Who told us we even had a right

To we?

WHO TOLD ME?

THAT I DESERVED ME?

YOU SAID YOU'D LOVE ME FLAWS AND ALL

BUT I DON'T EVEN LIKE MY WRONGS

HOW CAN YOU LOVE

WHAT I HATE?

WE ARE NO LESS THAN OPPOSITES

ADMIT IT

WHO TOLD YOU TO GIVE ME

SO MUCH ATTENTION

HOW DO I KNOW IF YOU'RE NOT

SATAN'S APPRENTICE?

I DO NOT FEAR US

I JUST FEAR ME

WHY DO YOU SEE PERFECT?

AND OTHERS SEE A CRITIQUE

WE ARE FORK AND SPOON

BUT DON'T DESERVE THE SAME PLATE

SO HOW IS IT THAT PIZZA & PANCAKES

BE EATEN WITH THE SAME TASTE OF FATE?

Royal Penis

He was the victim of a pedophile assassin

And the prey of a sin

Just a youth in his prime

Ready for dreams of no restriction

So while you unzip your pants just for a quick fix

And allow your limp dick to penetrate a young boy's body

As he fights back with anger

And the hatred inside of him glows

Like puberty when it grows confident

You sick fool, how dare you

Coerce a child to become your Uno card

Your bingo, such lingo

You are a fallen angel

And even if it were a young girl

I would still hate your intentions

For you murder a generation

Just by raping one dimension

But I can see that you are heartless

And you operate on violence

You promise a safe finish if they sacrifice innocent silence

And in return you receive nothing but a bounty on your head

In fact, justice probably is on your side

So many crooked cops that you don't even need to hide

But I know one thing

You will not escape the punishment of God

And I hate the way you kill Martin Luther's dream

And I hate how you anger me with the stroke of your penis

Your inner genius was never present

You should research what your gene is

See daddy wasn't so nice

And you saw all of it directly

The way he shattered her rib cage

Domestic violence to her belly

It makes you sick to your stomach

That he touched you when she was gone

And when he committed suicide

You felt he left you all alone

No closure

And so you mentally punctuate every possible

Fresh wound

Still not being satisfied with any answers

Your father abandoned

Do you realize that this is the same circle?

If you're caught

You'll become someone else's origami in prison

And if you retire early

You too will be a suicidal sin

It's a good thing I had a chance to read this diary

Now maybe I can save you from this sick anxiety

Where children are enslaved by an enslaved confused mind

And revenge is so sweet that it will agitate time

but it's a good thing I had a chance to read this diary

It would be easy to blame society

But this all was assisted

The devil killed chivalry

Effortless

Just as I was summer cleaning, I noticed an obsolete occurrence

And fixing it was irrelevant to the energy I saluted; foolish-ness

This guy which I was building a fantasy dream with, collapsed

I realized

He was far

Too ignorant

To love

And giving me his sweet personality, was never

Enough. No common sense breathed upon his mind

And victory was only subtracted with a piece of mine.

I tried

Patience

But it did

No good

Unborn love

Wishing release

I could

But I never seen it coming because I felt so unattended to – like

Even just a fiend could provide sufficient principles, but time

Wasn' t enough for him to know she. By the time he cried wolf, there was no me

SILENCE

My fetus should have been aborted long ago

says America.

For women are the underdog,

says America.

But I bet your big "A" is smaller than it boasts

and that the generic laws you possess choke like white men hanging
from ropes.

(joke?) No laughter now.

I guess that is what happens when a black woman decides

not to stay silent.

In some people it cuts deep,

but for others it's breaking tyrants.

The Lord is my witness and my mouth has been guided.

Peace sign to the skies

NO MORE SILENCE

Dosage 2: Outside In

Black Ruby

In my hand

I seen it coming   I
watched it glisten

Justice-less   An
image so familiar

Potential eye candy   with
its unsolved mystery

Hardened

Progress

By force

Faith

Silenced   You Exist

Love over

Non-shining

Hate

Diamond

Black Beauty

The edges were sharp   Such
a slave of thought

Needle in a haystack   Yet
brave of hearts

Poisoned & contagious

Pacifier

Heavily involved in his/her daily activities

Knowing that you just want what's best

Like an arrow through the chest

It would be

To watch your own seed

Break away its own branch

And plant its own tree, drifting like sea

You cannot teeth them forever

There are times when they must fall face first

And no matter how much it hurts to watch the pain

Regurgitate their innocence, breaking down their ignorance

Yet, building wisdom it

Has to be done

For in life there are no refunds

Love them with your faith

And hug them with passion

Sometimes they grow distant

From the morals you taught

And sometimes they turn out

Opposite of what you prayed about

Negativity will grow mold on the tongue

But you can't go backwards

Just to fix what's done

There was a time when you should have

Stayed up countless nights changing diapers

And times when you took them to school and practice

When you argued and fought

And when you laughed and cried

When you lived life in pure love

And when you died trying

But even with a mouth of memories

And a mind of hope

You'll never want to be the only one

Holding on to this rope

A string of dedications, survival, flaws and clichés

The birthday, birth place

The image in the frame

Just one day you would hope

That you made the right decisions

And if you didn't you would hope

That you could do it all again

But in the end

You will have to let the pacifier go

And if they know where they came from

They will acknowledge it

The sword is double-headed

Farewell my college kid

It is no longer cancer
Nor is it the war on terrorism

It is no longer black

Nor is it white

It is no longer the atheists

Nor is it the Christians

It is no longer hidden

Nor is it heard

It is no longer AIDS

Nor is it earthquakes

It is no longer the sky

Nor is it the ocean

It is no longer the whispers

Nor is it the cries

It is no longer the poverty

Nor is it the time

Lies

False

Untrue

Don't believe everything your eyes hear & your ears see

Question false prophecy!

Pennies of Quality

(In a fourth grade classroom)

Kelly: My pennies has more quality than the media

Teacher: What do you mean Miss Kelly?

*Class stares in confusion as Kelly stands up with her box of pennies

"I am afraid that specific music artists don't follow the "In God We Trust" and the radio doesn't play Lecrae and Lupe Fiasco enough. Not as if they are excused, I could be wrong but now it seems everything is the same. All videos on television show nude and rude things. It seems to me that entertainment all has mood swings. If the money isn't coming then they sacrificing dreams. Some say that our parents should do their "job" and turn it off. But it wouldn't even matter because I still see enough! Then what? Should they lock me in a cage and not feed me? Should they just play the game of teamwork, Mario, Luigi? Advertisements on the streets with hidden messages just to sex sell, and children imitate it just to experiment with themselves."

***Teacher tries to interrupt, but Kelly speaks louder

"My pennies have more quality! They do not have

expiration. I believe in value and I just don't get it. How can something so amazing be so damn pathetic?"

***Teacher: Miss Kelly that is ENOUGH, come with me, I am taking you to the office immediately!

"Well I'm sorry Mrs. Fritz, but you know I have a point. Did you know that during recess, your son is outside smoking a joint? Did you know that even cartoons are erasing the minds of the young and screwing up their lives, and we just blame no one? I know this may be rude, but I'm just not sorry. If we can't speak like they do, then who are we? My pennies have more quality......"

*Class applauds as Kelly is carried away to the office of no return

GPS

Driving a bugatti is the founded cure

for cancer

So every time we wake up

We in a world of lost answers

And I can make this run on

Likeastudentwhofailedbasicenglish

Cravingforthebasicknowledgetounderstand

Basiclogic

Insufficient funds support the drive of my wheel

And the smell of my engine releases fumes that kill

But still, I am happy

With the world beneath me

Green goblin in my pocket

I guess my intentions are greedy

I sex the world with my genius of knowledge

So above stupid, I turned away college

I can never get lost in this prediction

If the world is ending, I am the angel of the century

To hell with those who struggle

And to hell with those in pain

I just kiss my wood grain

And seduce the cold game

I'm on path yes

And you just don't know

I reject all help

And lip kiss selfish blows

So if I'm a sucker for oral

Then I'll come like a peasant

I love to brag about my glory

It's a flesh eating parasite

The way it bites and bleeds me

Nourishing desires unworthy of believing

Punctuations of a victim embedded in minds of

liars

In hate of all desires, God. Protect. Society

Violent Happiness

I punched the hel_ out of satan

For trying to fight one-on-one with me!

Knowing I got God as the commander in chief

Of my army

And that was simply funny

But for others it may not be so easy

I'm not bragging, I'm just grateful that I succeeded

I live with no regrets

Even with the biggest error of the century

But a broken Picasso to me

May be someone else's pretty

Forgive me

For smiling all the time and loving it

More than I love the hate on your face

My happiness is violent and it will do a

Drive by on your entire place

As I, shoot you with cupid

And I murder you with love

Well, I guess my aim isn't good enough

Because if it was

The entire world would have violent...happiness

Spacebar

What if the Bermuda Triangle was an escape into a world free of war and terrorism?

And the guns of violence became the peace of silence and we could reach one teach

one. If there was an easy exit would you pass through or pass? Hit escape or backspace?

I guess that would depend on if you were using a Mac or a PC. A cassette, CD, or mp3.

Welcome to the space bar, where thoughts

RUN

WILD

And we drink beverages that gravity cannot control, where the chemistry of your body

will caps lock your soul.

And how dare you power me off, I do not sleep well.

My master is hypnotized by a world of deep spell…

Dehydrated Intimacy

Franticly open, I carry myself by the handle

Knowing that this is what lovers must do

Stubborn to the realistic circumstances right before me

I gawk at myself in the mirror

No sweat and no tears left to even piss fluids

If there is rapture, then it is happening now

She must've been taken by angels before it fell to the grown

I can no longer exert the same efforts that I used to

Before it came easy, but now it seems an illusion

Has become my intuition and what I once had

Has become my contradiction

The depiction of a good thing, all I needed was a wedding ring

But fire flames and impatient ways

Broke the lion inside the cage

I used to drip love from the faucet

And he would drink it like H2O

I would give him goose bumps, with the voice

In my throat

But I knew something was off key

The anorexic lady couldn't sing

The fat lady cliché thing, rested far too mean

The entire relationship was bent dead out of tune

And I couldn't figure out why I was hugging myself

He had left me there with nothing else left

How stupid of me to give, and never to receive

So much for intimacy

Alone by Noon

When I would just hold her hand in pure insanity

It felt like life would drop from beneath me

Not that she was driving me crazy, but that

She would become my sanity and without her, I was pitch black

Back into the circles of "I don't want it"

And pressures of what a quick fix would do for my need of a replacement

The urgency I yearned for, when every time I slipped, all the other women fled

But these days were so different and she stayed

I think now I don't know how to love this woman

Because I expected something different than what I thought

I had coming

But I know that she deserves a king

I am just not sure if what she needs is me

What does she want from me?

Her eyes burn me with gifted embraces

And her presence is so vivid like a gun to my throat

When I didn't want to cope with the death of my brother

And my mother got sick and left me with no goodbye

I had nothing, but a loaded gun

She took it away and I fell numb

It was the first time I had ever felt love in my ribs

This woman wasn't the typical

My lady was for real

Mirror Wishes

You know when humans throw pennies into a fountain

In hope that someday their wishes would come true?

I never saw the purpose

Guess I'm behind on that too.

I gaze into a human made mirror and I notice

How much dependent I am

On myself.

At the blink of an eye I sensed a tear

Fall

Behind my mirror of wishes I am nobody

And no one cares to learn about my society.

I sleep with the stars and I sing with the moon

Yet, I am not emotionless like the depictions

On human televisions.

I despise being myself at times

If I was black or white I wonder if I'd be happier

I often dream about these interactions

And it seems as if those humans are so much better than me

They would just shoot me down if they assumed that I would change…

Never mind, I better not say that

I'll just dance with my mirror

At least that's where it's safe at.

Maybe I should take a risk

If I created a mirror big enough for the world of earth to see

I wonder if they would face the face they would be forced to acknowledge…

Unofficial

Your eyes remind me of delicate compounds

As they dissolve into the multi levels of my mind

And I feel as if time is constantly racing against mine

To the extent in which I cave in, like a baby's hand.

But this distance is like live footage of chemotherapy

And I can't kill this disease with the best of me!

I can't stand not being next to you

And I break like time capsules

My heart is so thick

But it leaks layers without you.

I been patient about the whole thing

The best things in life are not free

Because if I just had one chance

I'd pay for you with me

And I know that you've been hurt before

But I'm dying to be the drug of

Everlasting love and you can feign on me

Until we both spin the sun 180 degrees

I need you

Don't make me be stuck in the friend zone

Let our souls intertwine

Give me you to take home

I don't need you for the sex

I fell in love with your faith

If you like me as a friend, you should love me as a soul
mate.

Frustrated

How do you know if it's time to stop?

Do you devour yourself internally due to another's wants
and needs?

When do you acknowledge that today is the last time -

That you will give them a chance?

Like it's okay to forgive

But how long must you go until you continue to -

Slice your own throat?

Or bend over backwards

Just so somebody else can stroke....

Their own ego?

Well whenever you find out

Please let ME know

How much is enough

What is too much

And how to let go

John Doe

I see you in my future as I rise –

Taking your hand and painting with it

A perfect picture of vivid colors and ground breaking thoughts

MR DOE

I love your mysterious intentions and how you play mind games

That quivers every muscle in my body only to find out

I'm holding you.

And with every verb and syllable I silence you with magnitude

Curious of your hidden meanings and the silver lining of your manhood

MR DOE

But how am I to know if the hand that you are holding out

Is real?

That a part of me is missing due to a force field made to kill

And what if there is no escape and I have loved you with amnesia?

Then we shall lay your heart to rest, I won't need that either

MR DOE

Who are you?

And what have you done with me?

As soon as I am well again, I'll pour my corpse some tea.

DEAR GOVERNMENT: SHUTDOWN

Demonic enough that Egypt is engaging in this raging situation

Where faces are on the pavement and fire is digesting places.

How you gone tame all those people? You gone start another war?

Where bloodshed is the norm and peace is abort.

Snort disaster through the nose, I smell it all like a quick fix.

You the government is in this, so SHOW me how you gone fix this.

I'll be surprised if people listen, is nothing important until your dead?

If it's the truth anc hierarchy doesn't like it, they put a price on your head.

Mysterious codes are being found in pockets of homicide victims

And those on higher pedestals are destroying MLK's mission.

This country is in detention, we at a race against the clock

And the republicans are selfish in contagion with a lock

Placing strain on families who earned their spot, shooting down all realities

And recreating slcts, where unity is more distant and equity is numb.

We can't agree on a budget, so the government will run.

Republicans want to eliminate 317 million

On health clinics for women? You renege on commitment

800,000 employees affected, countdown to 12am,

No longer a paycheck. America you upset me, you have raised

Such anger. My stomach cannot feast on this infected train-

Of mistrust, disgust, greed, money, and blame.

Even the military families are in such distraught

How you deny the ones who fought with their mouths full of shots.

Yet you too good to get your hands dirty, and now we are so corrupt.

I'm not a politician but I know enough.

On the television, constant news, this just a tug-a-war

Pulling strings like puppets and feeding the public nothing

But a temporary shut up just so we can shut the hell up.

All over the internet penetrations that finger your mind and

Leave your accomplishments behind like a never ending circuit.

America isn't civil; this place is just a circus.

We pledge allegiance to this flag but I really don't see

The beauty, in my eyes it's just blind sight, jealousy and scrutiny

Seven more hours, six, and then five,

Four, then three, then two, and uno.

Back and forth countdown

Mouths filled with pollution.

Hearts covered with sinful intentions

And lies far beneath the obvious that the people been living.

In 1995 Clinton and the republican congress couldn't agree

So the system shut down and gave abortion to our economy.

This seed we were given has been mistreated like domestic cases

Being raped by each other, embarrassment in sour taste.

God forgive this sour dough, for we know not what we do,

If we don't prioritize and regulate, EPA won't investigate,

And there will be no social security, tax refunds, or state disabilities,

No department of education and other necessities.

So citizens wait in front of computer screens and TV's

Zombies by force, cause they controlling all wants and needs.

Mentally screwing the nation and giving birth to a demon.

I'm not angry, but I feel sorry for the oxygen we all breathing.

And Obama says that he doesn't want this shutdown to prosper

But there are simply some people, who can't risk losing another dollar,

Families to feed, and single homes with no fathers.

And I'm not a politician

But it doesn't take one to know

That earthquakes, tsunamis, and disasters aren't caused on their own.

The negligence to this earth has been so like slavery.

And the waste we produce is so unsavory.

That's the least to speak about, not including world violence and discrimination

The world is like a vagina, with all these fingers penetrating.

And no I'm not a hero, never heard of the word perfect

But I'd rather not be screwed, America should be a virgin.

And I know this takes patience and a lot of progress

But I can smell a conflict every time we see success.

You know the rumors about 2012?

Well yeah, all of this war is only complementing it.

I don't believe any of it, because my faith in God is too

Magnificent. Obama is just a black president, but he is still just human.

I'd rather live on the moon than to bathe in this sewer.

And I know this takes patience and a lot of progress

But I can smell a conflict every time we see success.

And I know this takes patience and a lot of progress

But I can smell a conflict every time we see success.

Dosage 3: Just a View

Airplanes

Let us pray

As we jump off the mountains of fear

And dive into the heavens of bravery

Where the wolves of the night

Become the peacocks of the afternoon.

Let us wait

As we purchase freedom out the stores

And dress up our insecurities

Like all the movie stars.

Let us feast

While we synchronize our blessings

Like time wearing tons of armor

And nothing can stand against it.

Let us dream

Like Martin Luther King

Oprah

The working c ass and everything in between

Let us fly

Tell the world the sky is NOT the limit

And we can go as far as numbers

Infinite digits

Airplanes

What if I was such a square that I compared to the stares of perceptions created

Not by me	A voice
Society	Success
Enemies	Loyalty
Haters	Adventure
Liars	Repentance
Aliens	Vision
Racist	Answers
Sexist	Leadership
Rapist	Knowledge
Media	Dedication
"friends"	Service
Parents	Mercy
Sickness	Grace
Hypocrites	Honesty

BOX SCREEN

false prophets	Peace
government	Faith
teachers	Power
leaders	Dignity
priests	Forgiveness
religions	Patience
sinners	Love
pretenders	wisdom
winners?	With

What if I knew that I was more than the statistics and needed God to provide me

Legally Black

Nowadays I guess I would be considered
In my element
Since my rich brown skin is no longer a sin
And the thickness of my thighs aren' t only
Perceived as a baby making machine
As if I birthed the baby boomers era itself.
Like I can shoot out countless eggs and
Just devour pain when it hits me
And like I shoot out life like a semi-automatic
With no problem, even if my bullets had no name
But nowadays I suppose I' m respected
For the quality of my brain.
The length of my education
And the produce of my name.
Every decimal of my existence is black
Even my flesh and bone
This white man' s world doesn' t see much
Other than this shade
No pigment and no cerebral distinctions
Exist
And though I breathe human air
I exhale the same stale nonsense.
Sometimes it is hidden beneath the teeth
Of those whose words forbid to speak

And leak upon the brownish cheeks
Of those who fell so foolishly.
But nowadays I can sit upon a classroom
In a majority white school and still
Raise my hand and be called on
Even if I'm chosen to represent my whole
Ethnicity.
Yes professor, do call on me!
I am sure I can speak for all the Negros
Or yes professor, do call on me!
So I can feel special
Outside of your pity
Am I wrong for being right -
For such assumptions?
In your eyes, I am sure
This is all falsehood
Like I receive equal pay like the white women
And even though we all were not able to vote
Once upon a time
Somehow black became the penny
And white a silver dollar.
It's better than being a zero perhaps
And maybe my husband is the president
Somewhere in the next
I guess I'm legally black
No longer a felony by birth

No misdemeanor by worth
And no homicide by curse
I love these laws
But I hate the way they contradict.
Yet, since things are so upside down
I guess its" wrong" to be white
If I' m legally black
Then it' s still wrong to be right.

Hand Gestures

Hands in the air and throw ya sets up

Really?

I never supported why colors of the rainbow

Could cause a gang war.

How does something so biological

Turn into something so suicidal?

With the flicker of a few fingers the world will gain a statistic

Someone will lose tonight

And others will feel uplifted

The power of revenge

Just a set of numbers, alphabets and variations

Maybe a few stars and bad connections

But with low reception

There will be a blackout

Maybe a bad drug deal

Or miscommunication at the trap house

But everybody likes to blame society

And is that not quite correct?

Must we treat the streets the same way

We do sex?

If you go out unprotected you bound to get tested

And if you careful you still got idiots who finger your morals

Life is worth more than a shade

And a struggle doesn't guarantee fame

But neither does stupidity

By all means, do learn the hard way

If all you want is money

Then rob the world's bank

And tell me if that's hard enough for you

Show me you don't fear

And tell me how you could have me killed

I just know one thing

I don't chuck up any deuces

I use two fingers, no parallel

And chuck the crucifix

Cause when you value nothing

You kneel to all means

So if this is the life you lead

Acknowledge its true genes

You can't birth a lie

Unless you succeed in screwing your dreams.

My Skyline

Purple and orange paintings stream across the sky's backboard

Like fighting swords and lightning bolts of surprise meteorites showers

Tomorrow may be extremely windy

The scent of the lakefront vibrates my nasal cavity

I embrace the lights and the fast cars that drive me virtuously

I love it

At night the buildings unite in harmonious visualizations

Taking my eyes for granted with its pretty display

I dare not look away

Outside of the violence and the irritating hood stories

That all of us lived by or witnessed at some point

This is me and my genes have bled

From this pool, in THIS place

I will not forget where I am from

When I proceed to deliver success

Like my present, my future will stress my past transitions

And this skyline deserves my attention

I took my first steps on this Chicago soil

Hell, I gave birth to poetry here in the city world

So if tomorrow isn't pleasant and the skies turn gray

Just remember the second city, reborn from unforgiving flames

And when my grave is set in stone

Do tell the world to bury me home…….

God's Eye

Direct

Teary Eyed

Watchful

Forgiving

Merciful

Powerful

Sharp

Dominant

Creative

And inside of it you will find

A map of what life is supposed to mean

Beyond the bible

And the dreams

The hopes

And the failures

With no contact lenses

Nor glasses

No magnified defiance

RELIABLE AND TRUSTWORTHY

WITH HIS EYES

HE HEARD ME

Regardless of

If society looks down upon you and the new advice
sounds like

Old stories

When family goes Casper

And strangers seem more like flesh

How others will perceive you

While many deceive you

With ridiculous excuses

And horrible attitudes

Accepting tides of water

And tolerating mountains of residue

Training yourself to win

But accustomed to lose

Delivered from anxiety

Yet receiving blank knowledge

That water fountain drinks you

This life is not promised

Say goodbye to regrets

And hello to regardless

Love Rush

They came armed

I had nothing to protect me

I had my mind and my dignity

I was ready

One broke in, the other was unexpected

Knocked me off my feet

No longer an easy checklist

I fell faint to confusion

A target for competition

How easy it is to love twice?

Is it just as hard as loving once?

I was crushed

No idea what the next step would be

Maybe I needed to surrender instead of shooting back

When they attacked me, I knew it was a trap

I just wondered how long it would be, *before they sold each other out for me*

Above Under

I walked into the room and saw myself lying on the floor

No pulse

Her beauty had gone pale and her smile still glowing

But I just knew this was a dream

I awaited the exit to wake up

Why have I watched myself lay stiff on the cold hard
wood?

I fetch a blanket but it dissolved right through her body

Hitting the ground

This dream was turning quite upside down

I frown

Sick to my stomach, this was no longer interesting

I look to the left wall where a mirror stood untouched

I gasp

These clothes are not just mine!

They are hers and I had copied her image completely

Was I just as dead as she? It appears she had been
wearing me!

In panic, I proceeded to dial 911

Not even the obvious things were a part of what I had become

The phone slipped through my thumb and rumbled the floor.

My asthma started to kick it, but this time

I did not want my inhaler as I fell to my knees

One person's nightmare, another's fantasy dream

Pitch black, all black everything

I glance over my right shoulder and somehow

She was gone

I cough up what seemed to be a ball of paper

Words inscribed on it that I could not read

With such saliva and mucus glazing it like a treat

I peek downward

A pencil piercing my flesh like homicide

I spit up what was supposed to be blood

But verbs and nouns have released themselves like alphabet soup

As if reality was a cartoon

The paper unfolds and I collapse like a broken mirror

I guess you live by the passion

And you die by the pencil

I have lived my life high and I've witnessed life

Low

Witnessing my own death like a bible verse

Do not mourn over me

For I have died poetically

All I ask is that my fellow poets

Carry my legacy.....

R.I.P

Karate Sex

Just laying in the bed with my legs open isn't enough.

Body heat doubled in slices I am dying to absorb-

Fiddle with my dignity like a fighter to its sword-

And herd my cattle like a stolen treasure.

This is serious,

make me speak in increments I cannot measure.

Physically provide me with attention that my lips no longer
stutter

Seduce me mentally on levels higher than o-zone

So that I crumble with the embrace of your tongue.

This is critical,

Shatter me with respect and carry me with wings

Hold me next to your heart

As you kick it to me deep

A legend in the sheets

But a man who values the ring.

This is different,

No baby mama stupidity

No one night stand

No friend with benefits

No Fairytale king on my land

We can engage in karate sex

AFTER YOU FINGER ME.

Natural Vision

I am not as blind as you think I am

By impulse I digest your arrogance and spit it in your face like mucus

How rude of me right?

Please dear, do take your own advice

When I was nice, you did not allow it to manifest your mind

When I was giving, you took advantage of all of me

When I was fed up, you left

Now you're thirsty as ever to get back what was never yours

I'll die by the sword before I commit suicide to you

I couldn't be with you if I wanted to

See you

Are stuck inside the pupils of a child during puberty

I growl like a lion and stand like a tree

Don't you dare knock on this wood

I attempted to do what a good person could

You are not worth a grudge

No time

No way

No more mistakes

I saw my future before you but with you

I can't

I am sorry that I could not suffice

But next time, please child...take your own advice

Just a View

We bulldoze forest preserves to the selfishness
of mankind

And to the drop of a dime, we neglect our
canines and felines

For a little bit of the green

We seem to do so many things

Without understanding the most simple means

When nature is more kind than the many wars we
start

And when birds sing with more heart than those
who sell out

Is it one for all or all for nothing?

When you live life running

You die on your stomach

At this point you watch it all hit you directly

You say what goes on over there

Doesn't affect me

There is no such wet dream

But this is just a view

There is a new war coming

And the target

Is you…

Dosage 4: Competition with Self

ROAD RAGE

Shackles of glass shiver the concrete
Like a death trap waiting to explode
As if the blood inside the nose would
Trickle, down your clothes

Ask yourself
How much would it hurt if you were in the front seat?
Fiercely thrown forward like a drum beat
As you aggressively wet the dashboard with the sweat
From your cheeks

Silence is reassured and everything goes black
Now time is pushed back like a Negro on a white clock
And death seems so certain like blood on cotton swabs
Regretful

Like it was your fault that you decided to drive
But it wasn't your fault that the other vehicle
Was manufactured by a bottle of Hennessey
You can't always see everything

Because if we had seen everything coming
Then we would reverse the bullets and diseases
The robberies, murders, and negative speeches
The demons and the blood sucking leaches

Which is worse?
Living a fantasy or dying a reality?
What if in both endings
You would still be on a battlefield?

I wonder how that would feel
To reverse such hurt
To go back into time and grab a hold
Of the seconds

I guess that's what you call
An abstract blessing
Is it still road rage
When you did everything to avoid it?
Or is it a raged road, infected with corpses?

ONE MORE CHANCE

Just to read a book

To make another wish

To bring back grandmother so we can do
another kiss

Just to go to school again

Just to change someone's life

Just to turn back the hands

And turn
away from all the fights

Just to live again

Just
to laugh and learn to love

Just to listen

Just to open arms and hug

Just enough

Just to breathe and not to die

Just to believe   Just
the opposite of a lie

Just to expect   Just to cherish what I had

Just to pray

Without my children being afraid

Just to succeed

And just to fall again

Just give me one more chance to be ...

Just a better me

ZEBRA SKIN

Not to be cliché

But are zebras white with black stripes or

Black with white ones?

What if society was two toned?

Would there still be racism?

Like if you white folk would be literally half black all in one serving

Them black folk be Caucasian like a snowman

Could we handle it?

It seems it's too much to deal with when we are all

Different

So what if we were all the same

Could we learn to live united?

Without being each other's bait?

Cause equality is a fictional book

That no one chooses to read

And if that's the case

Then peace is all a dream

I suppose zebra skin

Wouldn't change a thing…

BLACK RAIN

Allowing the se f to be curious to the unknown

Could cause ycu your life

Opening your mouth just to taste what could be candy
rain

Fail

It humiliates your tongue, burning every desire until
there is nothing to smile about

Like spoiled milk on the tongue of an adult

Of course a new born child wouldn't know the
difference, they would just frown perhaps

You spit it out

This is not what you expected from the heavens

Or had it even traveled from that direction?

The rain fall has become heavy like black diamonds

They sting your skin and bruise your mind

Too much thinking and too much confusion

Puddles of black rain freeze on the concrete like black
holes

You remove yourself

Better safe than sorry

Looking to the skies you question this behavior

Had the sky people started a war like Avatar?

This must not be healthy for the life beneath the stars

You feel yourself drifting away slowly

The movement around you freezes as well

And you hold out your palm to catch one of the black

glaciers

You shatter

Splashing to the ground along with the rain drops

You have become one of them

No longer the one on top

For now...you have yet to be walked on

SIGN LANGUAGE

As a child I realized how different communication was

Yet I did not understand

What's a mouth with no words and an ear with no sound?

What's the sky to the ocean?

And a tear to the ground?

The mumbles of a misinterpreted minority

Just a struggle to dream like the majority

Dodging obstacles that shred you like bad paper

I am no disease

You do not have to treat me like a freak

No alien of me

Xenophobic

I am inserted in life to become assertive

For those who are afraid to speak up, in fear of false judgment

Thou shall not kill

Emotionally and physically

If time was promised I bet you'd murder infinitely

But please do not ask for what is not your own

And don't expect a blessing that has already been gone

I breathe like you do and we all die someday

But before reality matures you

Know that I count too and this is by no means in comparison to you...

Hazards

Just like a headache

Shambles and loose intuition

Wishing upon a star that is too distant to
grab

I scratch at it crabs

With no intention to become cleansed

If life is always this hard

I'm not determined to win

And who are you to tell me

I should give a damn

With this pen in my hand

I should contaminate my wrist

In a world filled with piss

All you can do is dismiss

Leaving all those who love you

On a satellite dish

In search of a signal

But they'll never find it

Too toxic to be touched

Self destruct

Too giving to give love

Vulnerable Hazard

A DAY AWAY

When is it okay?

I mean, if I can't intellectually penetrate you

How do you expect me to come?

You make my days seem so unsure

The way your mind fluctuates like a womb baby

And how your mindset rubs me like a genie trapped with no exit

I did not expect to be caressed incorrectly

It seems that patience has become my specialty

In a heartbeat

I tell myself this is not where I belong

Tomorrow is just a day away

And oh how I wish it was promised

Twenty four hours away from the storm

Time ticks slower than slow

A sunrise away from yesterday

And a moon lit evening caves in

Maybe one day I'll love enough

So much to fill the skies

A day away, too far from today

I hope that I can wait

For the rose petals and the fragrances

The surprise hugs and kisses

The actual meaningful quality of words

The compliments of beauty

Dignity of having a good thing

The compliance of a mastermind

Sacrifice of a king

The stability of a secure network

And the satisfaction of a dream

I just hope that I can wait for tomorrow

Even if all of my time

Had been borrowed by the last fool

And I die young from giving all my love

Away

If the day away comes and it arrives without meeting me

I hope I go to heaven so I can witness love equally

Although if this is where I am meant to be

A day away

Insanity

ZERO

The deposit of a massacre at its peak like dual war
between freaks in the sheets
Hits you like radiation between the legs of a woman
ready to let loose
Withdrawing from her most secretive ways and not even
ashamed
Forgetful memories rise above her control level like
bread in an oven
She gets hot and sweaty as she manipulates his head
game
Against the "bed frame", she licks her lips in pure
seduction
His body was like a sex symbol, rocky mountain heaven
With a gaze into his eyes like seven eleven
She looks him up and down like a time glass
So serious that it hurts to hold in all her frustration
No longer feeling she is on level nothing
Someone please make love to the kitty cat
It's been far too long and she doesn't plan to go back
He openly ignites her ambitious fires
Willing to explore her canyon like bears, lions, and tigers
She goes wild like a crowd at a basketball game
Who would have known that playing mind games would

lead to

A mental orgasm?

Dying to punctuate her sensitivity like hot flashes

Then the console crashes and everything relapses

You look upon the scoreboard and realize the game is
over

The ring on his finger puts him directly in the no no

You can now acknowledge his worth

ZERO

I KNOW ME

You know how you tell me you know
everything about me
But your actions seem to show me you
know nothing?
Like a chocolate truffle waiting to be
eaten...
Melting away like a finishing touch.
And when I anger you
Everything seems so easy to let go
And somehow my personality all of a
sudden loses worth
Like I'm not worth fighting for?
Well, of course you are entitled to
your opinion dear
Maybe I'm not worth it
I just never knew you were perfect......
Had I known this in the beginning,
there would be no end
I would have never given you a
syllable to breathe with.
What about when you expect the world
But you only give me dying oceans?
Or when I present you with loyalty
And all you see is frozen love
Like a blue ray television paused at
its most dramatic scene
The burden of an angel on a demon's
wing.

I know me

Even when the skies drop on my head in the form of hail

When the grounds rumble underneath me like bad headaches

Through all of the opinions and perceptions

Bad reception and harassment

And when cupid no longer has faith in me

When friends become a vacancy

Trust one thing

I
Know
Me

TRANSFORMER

At first I was able to enjoy your appearance without all the damaged
or unfinished paint jobs

Able to go full throttle until I felt my heart race like Nascars

A smooth personality and luxury at heart

The ways you caressed me mentally with your automatic start

But whenever you switched gears

I felt we were moving too fast

And that we would miss out on a tire rotation and finish last

Our rear view started to seem more like a distant fear

Utilizing the windshield wipers to push aside consistent tears

Just when I thought we had fought away all the bad guys

All of a sudden there is a recall

And what we have has become a free fall

Pedal to the metal

The breaks screech and it seems you are opposite of me

Our gas in on E

Yet we has driven full speed

Right into a brick wall

A diagnostic test could have saved us

I hate you

Look at what selfishness made of us

変圧器

KIN FOLK

Breed
Species
Type

Villain
Suspect
Hype

Breathe
Love
Life

Gain
Lose
Rights

Scatter
Like
Mice

Not
So
Nice

Stanger
Equals
Your own

Trust
No
One ?

WORLD WAR III

So Lebron James is king?

That's enough for me

To know that this damn hell hole will have a
World War III

 Religious denominations

In competition with the rest

That's enough to see

Planetary selfishness

The world will end then

The world will end now

False prophecy will knock a whole nation

Out

The president isn't black

Hell, the president is blue

That's enough to say

Who the hell are you?

Racism is gone

Freedom has arrived

That' s enough to say

Abraham is alive!

Sex is on Sponge bob

Sex is on deodorant

That' s enough to smell that

Quality is so odorless

This may be humorous

Hell, it may be simple

But it' s enough to know

Society is so sinful

This is not for saints

It is not for sinners

No matter how you see it

The world is not a winner

I write these words

And you get mad at me?

HELL, THAT'S ENOUGH TO BE

WORLD WAR III

Dosage 5: Lost In Perspective

IS IT LOVE?

Is it love that captures my heart, but not my mind?

As I pawn my emotions like a diamond, but for no profit

Because I'm just that generous. Us, black women are stains on the carpet,

The excess in the toilet and the stoop in the forest

For its no longer only the white man who raises his hand,

We are betrayed so often by our own men…women

Why tolerate the everlasting plate that he feeds you

No veggies, just beef, girl he feeding you cancer.

Too blessed to be stressed, or is it the reverse?

Put down on the ground has become his next curse.

The eyes of a sparrow, bone marrow, tea kettles

But battle after battle, incarcerated to the devil.

Misused and abused, you a man, then choose.

Stop walking in the shadow of other niggaz

And just tie your own damn shoes

Is it love when it hurts, is it pain when it burns?

Does it lie when it's real, will it cry when it learns???

MISTAKEN IDENTITY

So he is one statistic, he sees the outline of a very imperfect man

But in my case I may seem blinded by satan's plan. (What a hateful man)

These chemical imbalances have stirred up some destruction.

My identity has been mistaken for somebody long gone....

Eager to stick my hand out and be cut by knives,

But don't think I am the one who is presenting them!

People in this world treat each other like perpetrators...

who destroyed the body of Jesus.

The only difference is that we can't rise from the dead, unless we angels or demons.

I'm mad, I'm on edge, somebody give me a thesis...

So maybe I can write my own summery and do a little bit of research...

Maybe the world would listen if I created my own rebirth.

Listening has become extinct

and the only time I realize I'm alive is when I brush my teeth (why?)

Cause that's the only instrument that gives me power to speak...

An organism by voice...

This world has been swallowed, regurgitated, no moist....

Dehydrated on terms that we choose not to fix...

So when I die, I want my loved ones to know of my internal bliss...

Just so they understand that I refused to be the toilet to the devil's piss.

Remember this, cause when these worlds go...

I am lost no more... forget some wings.

I'm returning to the dirt that complements my pores.

So if I'm lost in this identity, this world is faceless and

I'm the enemy.

NON-EXISTENT VOICE

As if society doesn't enslave her enough by color,
and as if the struggle of this patriarchal world
doesn't force her to work twice as hard just to be acknowledged
from the glimmer of her soul to her battle scars...

Why should she have to feel so invisible to her significant other?
Trapped by repetitive syllables and silenced utters.
Stained in a way that excels beyond Microsoft word...
Underlined and defined by the power of her verbs...
However, no experience can capture one like this.
How can a dove so gorgeous be made to feel like a pigeon's
waste?
She calls out to God with tears beneath her face…
Refusing to shed them, tiresome of being sick and tired...
Your words don't mean anything to her unless AMPLIFIED!
Seriously, we've all been there before!
But when will she get the chance to not open the same kind of
door?

ERROR
Like a cocked gun, bussing its first nut… at a slut,
but there are no walls to penetrate.
So she breaks with any noise that he creates.
Fed up isn't even the word.
How can patience even exist in a body so tried -
when it has died deep inside, fighting to simply stay alive?
Yet the cries are over-powered by this word that's been misused,
excused, coughed on, diseased with no tissue.
Stabbed with no pencil and sketched with no stencil...
Love? How dare you speak of such…
Never knew that wanting security was asking for too much.

She keeps knocking until her knuckles bleed
Vulnerable, just fresh - in need of growth...a seed!
So voiceless to the point where she feels ignored,
yet a stranger embraces her more...and this confusion

rushes to her temple like a deal at Dollar General.
Everything she does seems to go down the drain,
from the way she loves him, to the faith she craves
And if days don't determine a way out, an escape -
How dare you get mad at her when she shows your face.
How bitter does it taste? Must not be so nice..

And all you have is excuses to govern your inexperience.
Excuses hiding your naive and all of your ignorance.
What if she has a right to get mad?
Countless times in the past, no lag, carrying loads of bagg...-age
Though she wishes no harm against you…
It's like being deaf and stabbing her eye sight with a pencil.
If she disappeared would she be transparent enough?
Or would you dare to pay attention then? In need of her
medicine…
Violated by gender, degraded by memory.
Enslaved by desire, in love's chemistry
Parallel to reality, yet perpendicular to this fantasy...
Decimated by insanity, destroyed through humanity

Buried within the depths of a soul's cry
Gone with the wind in the blink of an eye
Sigh
Time goes by like countless numbers
Voices unheard like suicide, bombers.

What happens when she is left with no choice?
But to look in the mirror and realize…
Her non-existent voice

Blue-N-Pink

Would it be so disrespectful to dress a newborn boy
In pink
A girl in blue?
Does a young cub begin life with such social identities?
Are butterflies actually beautiful?
Inner beauty is subjective and so are the patterns of life
Does a tongue speak truthfully?
Are tortures of terrorism learned or already known?

Well this one is
For you
Who think colors blend unselfishly
To you
Who knows the hue of success
Just as much as the shades of failure

For all the aborted seeds who had wings
But never a chance to sprout
Eager to be acknowledged
But not humble enough to figure life out

And this is to the me's
And the you's
The life of one confused
Sketched with all the pink
And blues

Always

It's the little things that make the bigger things

Matter

Had time been measured in increments of true value

No female would become the pitch fork of what is now

Only a tasty meal

As if the ice sickles from hell

Are realistic enough to proclaim one's worth

Fresh

Like bacteria at its peak investing its pure strength

Inside the minds of the weak

They who speak naïve words of temptation in thy ear

It must sound so good

But the truth is crystal clear

Weird

If God would have intended for such things

One organ would suffice and there would be no need

To have a heart nor brain

But it is all the same

Women are selfish beings

For holding back on all the sexual urges

For lacking perversion

And controlling what is and isn't urgent

Hopeless fate

Do wash these words away, I pray

Drown them in a virgin's bay

Symphony

I HEAR IT COMING IN WAVES   AS IT
CRASHES INTO THE SHORE
    WHEN AN OCEAN SPEAKS   ITS LIKE
INFINITE CRIES OF MUSIC
    NOT THE ILLUSIONS   BUT THE
WHITNEY HOUSTONS
    THE JESSE POWELLS   AND THE
KEVON EDMONDS
    EVEN NEW EDITIONS   AND
TONI BRAXTONS
    WHERE MUSIC WAS MORE   THAN
SIMPLY ACTING
    THE PASSIONATE OVERDOSE   OF
MYSTERY AND THE GENTLENESS
    OF LOVE   BEATING
PATIENTLY WITH BASS
    BUT ALWAYS ON TIME   WITH
WORDS THAT SOOTH
    THE MORE THAN SEX   THE
MORE THAN MONEY & HOES
    THE FAITH OF GOD   NOT THE
SELL YOUR SOULS
    I FALL TO THE GROUND   MY EARS
HAVE BLED
    THE TREBLE AND CLEF   HAS
MADE A WISH

IN THE BEGINNING   THERE
WAS DEFINITION
IN THE END   THERE
WAS ANYTHING
I OPEN MY MOUTH   I SPEAK
THE TASTE BUDS   ON MY TONGUE
MARINATED WITH   WHAT
WAS ONCE...SWEET
NOW BITTER   I DELIVER
HOW NICE IT WAS   I WAS
ONCE IN LOVE

WITH YOU

Beneath
the
Pen

Minerals of compressed wood

Water color

Lay rested underneath its companion

It doesn't take much to say

They carry each other away

There will never be a better lover

Inseparable by literature

The only way to impeach them

To ask God for a detour

Blind Again

Breathless cannons disengage me
Thoughtless actions irritate my kind spirits
Prejudice of the speechless
Jurisdictions of a simple minded moron
I grab my rib cage as it explodes desperately
Like fireworks on Independence Day
I salute the inner genius I once used to possess
Limitless as a nest constructed by America's strongest
bird
Murder
Like a crow you lurk black foundations on solid
concentrations
Ignorance in the making
Lord forgive them for they know not
What they do
And foolish pride arrests all jealousy like day break
Sending chills up your spine like three blind mice
Silence has scared you heartless
And until I find mine again....

I'd rather be blind again

Head Lights

Full speed he runs
His antlers as beautiful as a sculpture carved by
careful hands
Nothing will stop him now
He just birthed a new born fawn
Mating season is over but hunting season
Begins soon
He leaps into the forests in search of some bed room
At least this particular area hadn't been destroyed
by
Construction companies and conniving architects
A father is supposed to protect and provide
He knows this, even better than mankind itself

Times have changed
Society has made it harder for me to provide for my
family
I am in control
I was here first
He stumbles on the busy highway
His attempt to get to the other side
What happened next would change a bird into a fly
He stands there in miserable agony
His doe had jumped in front of an oncoming vehicle
to save him

The sacrifice of a lifetime

He wishes it was him, how would he raise his fawn alone?

Why would she sacrifice her own?

He kneels, it should have been me

He is tired of running so he waits

The rest of the traffic stops in awe

Normally they would continue to drive

I guess everyone can't live the American dream in flashing lights

Quick Sand

I did not want to be in this position

I never even asked for it

It came to me secretly like a gun reloaded

No longer could I understand what was placed before me

Something was forcing me to choose

Somehow I knew to distinguish love from the lust

When I tried to back away

I found myself in a black hole

Gawking at what appeared to be a missing layer of my soul

I was not familiar with this adjustment

This was too hard for me to handle

I did not want these feelings

Life is so much easier selfish

I'd rather be a shellfish

Secluded from the world and distant from love

How can something so unknown become the deposit of trust?

Confirmed

I felt it speak to me
A spirit
At that point in my life I didn' t want to go
Near it
It did not give me warning but it did invite itself
I felt trapped
How to distinguish an angel from a demon?
Maybe it was my time to go home
Or maybe karma was here to reap what I had
sewn.

The blood was on the wall
 Had I put it there myself?
Who would have known that such lack of faith −
Would become a plea for help?
I swallowed
It felt like I had eaten my own esophagus
My life was in danger and it was all so profitless
The years have turned and my sins have burned
thorns
I am nobody but the unknown

Lady Love

Living life like love's liberty leaves loneliness lost

And above all assets are ambiguous actions

Dying duets differ drastically, demanding dismantled dictations

Young yesterday yearns

Legacies listen like lies

Obliged obstacles only organized

Voices vibrate virtuously via verbal vindications

Every ethical entity exaggerated, exploited, excused

In black and white

Why is lady love so abused?

Is it the complexity of her mindset?

Or the ambitious nature of her intelligence?

The motivation of God in her decisions

Or the color of her skin?

In complication

Why is it so hard to love?

Ain't I lady enough for lady love?

133

Miss Me with That

I suppose one can only take so much blasphemy

The root of all evil is pride

Thou shall not boast in the face of it

I say I'm sick of being sick of you

To the point where my stomach turns over like over cooked meals

And it's always easier to walk away

Then you're stuck with little closure

But I guess I'd rather spit than kiss up to you

Miss the way I smile and how beautiful my mind is when it's at its best

The way I light up an entire room when I acknowledge my own worth

How I stood up for you when even your own kind turned about face

Or when I was patient with your ignorance, naïve and dumb mistakes

Me who did the best I could do

Me that went to school, worked double, and loved you

Me that prayed for a yes, even when God showed me no

Me who has to let go

With all you never gave me, now somehow you find me
engaging

Miss me with that...

Dosage 6: Wet-N-Dry

BUTTER BED

I grip the sheets to gain balance

It is hard for me to move through the fabrics

So I sit there and analyze the situation

I regurgitate the sweat through my pores

As it slithers down my limp body like murder

I open them up as the air hits

I gasp

I couldn't understand why I had been laying on a damp

Mattress

This was never expected

Some nightmare my life must be

What is this?

Who had made a fool of me...

On call

Get up and get ready

I can sense your mysticue

Through my teeth I taste your disgrace

From a distance

I get tired of seeing you everyday

You look sour half the time.

If you feel the same way

I respect your criteria

I'd like to have you near

But I'd rather love you from a distance

Directly, you're more in control of

EVERYTHING

And that's too much for me to swallow

From here, I have power too

And that's why I love myself

Because when others can't, I will

I cannot see our love through you

I only see an acquaintance

Plus we simply LOOK good together

You complement my beauty well

But truth be told

I'd prefer you to be on call

No full time job, just loving me if needed…

Your love is Quadriplegic

LESS THAN 60, MORE THAN 10

I feel like a winner

Guiding myself on an endless plane of self desires

With a few sprinkles of pain and icing made of trial and error

I know my history like an historic artifact

And no one can shape or mold

What I have already experienced

Some people like to tell me about myself

And my worth

How I smile too much and how I

Don't know how things work

I am not sorry

That I don't understand you

Though I apologize for what you are about to lose

Because you won't appreciate a thing like me

I was here at this point in life

Way before you stumbled upon my eye sight

You didn't bring in anything that I had never had

Before

You actually brought an arrogant stench that glows

With negativity

And now you wish to get rid of me?

Only a fool trades an hour glass for 10 seconds...

UNDER CONSTRUCTION

Envision a family portrait in a nice wooden frame

Everyone is smiling and posing for the camera in endless laughter

Memories

The one's that never last

A temporary fix to a lifetime of deceit, jealousy, pain, and loss

No way to photo shop the truth

Oh how you wish there were ways to fix the blemishes

The hidden faces behind the camera lenses, only to tell a fictional story

To the public eye, this family seems pleased and satisfied

To the actual eye, this family is segregated like male and female bathroom stalls

Beneath the family name is a diary of madness

Everyone pretty much stays to themselves

Nothing like the gigantic families you see on television

This is the reality with no flavor of love

Perhaps sometimes genetics isn't enough

Please be aware that this road is blocked off

There is a fine for those who trespass

These roads must be fixed

Or lives will collapse

As if a third plane hit...

WISHFUL THINKING

I wipe away the tear drops that my eyelids released

It felt like heaven's house warming to be next to you

Getting married at last, we were ready

The best kiss I had ever feasted upon

I awake in a cold sweat

You were not there!

I run downstairs with a lump in my throat

It was my heart

I could not swallow it for the breath of me

I snap out of it

Back to the red carpet at the wedding hall

Our relatives cheer in happiness as they take Kodak moments

I did not feel happy, I could not speak

I look to you and a stranger looks back at me

I tilt my head and it breaks as I watch my heart form on the floor

My neck had a hole in it

I wake up

You're ready to make love

Kissing me on the neck until I felt like giving up

I close the book, wishing she was me

I pick up my heart as I watch it sleep

ORIGAMI

I' ve folded my life into a paper airplane

Like arts and crafts all over again

Then the crease is never perfect, I
wrinkle like ironless

Not being good with my
hands is a mess

I can always see
the perfect image

But I can
never own the moment

I betray me

Sick to my stomach

My hands start to sweat and my
thoughts turn into vomit

I close my eyes

as if sight never occurred

My playing field is not the work of the talented

People excuse my skills for average

I die young

Fold my casket into an envelope and send it to some
nuns

Maybe that' ll give me a reason to *become*

FIRE HOES

Why is it that you cannot keep your eyes on your OWN paper?

I guess I am not supposed to trust you when you're not with me

Like you never seen a female before

It's like you go brain dead at the snap of a finger

And not even my best asset can keep you on track now

Cause your too busy on track used

You prefer a simple minded chick with a thousand loose screws

One who wants to buck for your change and brag about what ya'll got

You like em' thick in them places but petite in brain and heart

I get it boo

Gone ahead and chase ya "riches"

Later it'll be too late to dial my digits

I refuse to become the backboard to your game plan

I deserve a full breed, not a mixed breed abandonment

You are not worth the time of day

I've seen a million dudes and many of em' want to take your place

How dare you stare my ego in the face

And rape all of my support like it was just plan A

149

I've decided you are as worthless as this poem

Since you the topic and it has ya name written all on it

I'd like to love it for the moment, because this is the last of you

You get a pass, but next class, take ya trash with you

I don't need to burn ya clothes, you already need to fire hoes

LUSTFUL TRUST

When I wear my tank top you tend to touch me a little more

than usual

Like when my jeans hug my skin and my thighs seem three

dimensional

I bend over and you stare at that longer than into my eyes

But now I just started paying attention

Why is it that when we love making you tell me you love me in

double digits

Yet when we just spending time you'd rather watch ESPN?

Do I place you under Lifetime, Oxygen, or Shemar Moore?

You'd be gone a long time ago if I did

And to think that your sperm is where I want some kids....

Hilarious

I dare not place myself in agony

I don't know if I should deny your love or accept your lust

If I must, be evaluated by the auto-tune of my beauty

Then excuse me, because I have no idea what the hell I was

thinking

I must have blocked out all yo ugly and replaced it with pretty

Literally

DEEP DISH

I swallowed

It slid down my throat like bubble gum

Sticky on my tongue

had to prepare for

What would come

Whatever it was

I hoped that I could stomach it

Just a taste of it

Purposely a target miss

LET'S GO FISHING

It doesn't take a diamond ankle bracelet or a brand new car

I never asked for the money or a world of stars

What about words of encouragement or "baby you make me proud"

Why weren't you there when a boy first let me down?

To tell me I deserve the best and that you'd hold my hand

That you would be the best guy, second to God, that I ever had

And that even when you made me mad, you would still be…

Dad

What about basketball tickets, or a walk in the park

Show me how to fix a car or even how to break hearts

Some type of quality lesson, would have sufficed

But this sperm in my life, doesn't define its rights

I don't ask for much

I never did

Love me like mommy

The grand wish of a kid

No longer innocent, memories never forgotten

To move on with my life, with your trust in my pocket

Along with the lent and rusty pennies

If I could take back time

I wouldn't replace any

Being your child is like going fishing...

GYMNASTY

I like to play acrobatics with my
tongue

My body movement fits the
description of a snake

The jungles finest predator

In search for my prey

I lay within the rubble

Expectations are unpredictable

I smell fear

He is not ready to greet me

I standby

Eager to allow him to taste me

He backs away, this doesn't seem
safe

I take initiative as I wipe the
smirk off his face

Dominating his body

I make love to his blood stream

His immune system shuts down

This is all me!

And to think I would allow

Such a fine thing to walk past me

I had to be acknowledged

I like my gym nasty

SPEAK YO BATTLE

Open like openness
Speak upon the speaking
Do without the not doing
Laugh without the jokes

Judge like you won't
Win like a loser
Kill like a butterfly
Run like a cougar

Love like hate
Justice like war
Battle like scars
Die like hard

Never like forever
Try like black errors
Concentrate like feathers
Heaven without questions

Wealth with no bank
Go fish in dirty tanks
Lie with no rank
Forgive like mistakes

Dosage 7: Justice Served

Tick-Toc

Vulnerable to the sound of it-

Revulsion by sight.

Black and white elegance founded upon my life!

Just a little cub manifesting on this childhood-

In the presence of a sibling, sensitive to his demeanor.

Shot dead by his wicked intentions.

Submissive to my tears-

I release them like bad habits.

Some sibling you are, to cause terror so rapid.

To the confusion of my mother-

Not knowing what the cause was to my effect!

Trial and error led her to the voice of neglect.

Caught red handed, the culprit was just an analog-

He placed one before my young face; just to get a taste,

Of my sour apple face, misguided by the pace

Of the hands on the clock-

As they went TICK

TOC

EVEN WITH BARS

I salute you

Rapist

For being coward enough to use force

And slick enough to threaten death if I snitch

I acknowledge you

Hustler

For shooting my innocent next door neighbor

Three years old

And will never know what a diploma is...

I remember you

Traitor

Who walked out of our history

For a fantasy lifestyle

And a fast lane mystery

You surprise me

Justice

You're nothing like the constitution

The books you teach in schools

or the flag we pledge to

Even when your miles away

I'd never want to visit you

Subliminal

I'm sorry for what society did
to you

But you're the least innocent of
the two…

Time = Lies

Fireflies and tampons
She craves them both heavily
One for elegance
And the other for destiny

She bows down to the shores
And counts the waves as they crash
Blackouts come so sure
As if distance was perfect

She takes a nap beside the fire ants
As they reproduce next to her on the sand
There are no dangers on this land
Dishonesty had won again

A life full of premonitions
Imaginations
And fairytales
She watches herself sleep

Bones and all
When she becomes someone's guardian
Angel
The lies will fall off

Black History

Have you ever thought about it -

Or have you taken everything for granted?

The stories, the teachings, and the re-written documents on the internet

Is it possible for all truth to be in what they teach to the children?

What if plenty has been omitted and the naïve are senseless?

Who

When

Why

Must we believe everything we hear?

While they snicker and laugh at what we lack to know and fear

It is true!

History is black

Covered up by the mysteries carried upon the dead man's back

The negotiated limitations

And the corrupt penetrations -

That has robbed the legacy of -

Those who were colored

The sisters and the brothers...

The funny thing nowadays is

We take the vision from each other

D.U.I

Partly cloudy

Inside the outs

Opening the mouth

Like Niagara Falls and wishing wells

Pouring a water park inside me

Best amusement I ever had

No tickets or long lines

Just selfish nonsense

With friends

The ride home was even better

Foot on the gas pedal

The rest - don't remember

But that had to be the coldest night

Dear September

What happened to the winter?

Must've had missed the next few seasons

Life was much different

Never knew such a slow roller coaster

Could end complete existence

Verbal Phobia

SMH

LMAO

IDK

ROTL

FML

OMG

I'd rather just text you!

WTF?

2NITE

LOL

TTYL!

Now imagine spotting this language in an academic paper

If you don't know these abbreviations by now

Then you're simply out of order

Be aware of what your kids say

BYOB

TD2M

Get a clue, direct communication is long expired

Now it's simply email, websites, and text messages

Entertainment is now sexting

And fruitful is now sour

So how anti-social have you become by the end of the hour?

no warning – just a plea

But what does this really mean?

Guilty

Observant

You indulge me

Creative

You trespass me

Humorous

You laugh me

True
You class me

Explicit
You nasty

When you speak

You surpass me

Can you deliver?

Maybe…..

Are you a front?

I wouldn't doubt it….

I'm guilty

I'm looking for

171

someone who builds mountains

Not houses

I Survived

I was helpless
It was me against the root of all evil
And you of all people
Would subject me as a victim?
I should have known that you were too good to be true
The first time you gave me up and dropped me off
At a crack house
Like someone in they right mind would sober up
And make me their child
I guess you couldn't do it
That time
So you decided to keep me
Found out that child support could bring you dividends

I knew you couldn't have missed me
Genuinely
How does a child of such innocence
Get stuck with ignorance?
I cried to you
It was me or the new guy
All of your boyfriends came first
Told me you wish you had ya tubes tied
When I came to life...

I don't know if I should hate you
Or love you
How can you care for someone who created all your troubles?
I'm numb now
And people would love to get close
But I'm overdosed
The ones who supposed to love you the most
Kill you will hollow blows

Under my nose I feel an itch
Though my life was a lie
I became filled with rich -
sanitation because heaven's bacon had fed me
When suicide was calling

I was graced by His melodies
Lord please forgive them
And cure their sickness instead of me

I'd rather die on humble street than to die a lifeless bumble bee

The Best Revenge

Take two steps backwards

You missed an important part

Pick up your dignity

And replace your pride

Who are you seeking to impress?

You cannot continue to skip looking in the mirror

One man's tear drop is another man's pit stop

Go to work

You owe it to yourself

You wouldn't need revenge

If

You took care of your own stealth

Start worrying about your own

And leave out everybody else

Not Sorry

For my opinion

For my education

My wisdom

God's creations

For my pains and errors too

For my backbone, cheek bones, and color too

For my wins and my loss

My tears and my costs

My joy or my awe

For my strength

My vagina

Not my voice

Or my silence

For my heart, broken or mended

And my dreams nor my defenses

Not sorry for those who never gave me

A chance

Not for love or for friends

Not for life or death

Even for fame nor for wealth

Not for you or your media

The moment I said NO....

I defeated you

The Power of Green

This is not for the marijuana feigns

This is for the pastures that we destroy

And you wonder why the deer run directly towards the

headlights

The price of mother nature

When a nation listens to satan

What happens when nature turns on mankind?

When no army squad can protect us

And no plan will survive?

Have you always underestimated reality?

No man made weapon can overcome

The very grounds we walk upon

What if nature said it was done?

Tell me where in the hells...would the good world run?

Seduced

Open doors

Shallow nights

Weeping willow

Frost bite

Painted silhouette

Gazing in the sun

When a stranger intends

Success to run

By moon and night

No wolf shall howl

By silent eyes

An owl dare smile

If pressure hits

No target must

To each its own

A lustful touch

Dosage 8: Black & White

He Was Courteous

Temptation was penetrating my mind
as I let it seduce me.
Trying to resist this mental sickness
was like trying to cure AIDS.
I was full blown, no appointment needed,
and if life was straight sex and was edible...
I'd eat it.
Hypothetically speaking...tongue marinated in metaphors.
I sat back on the couch,
mind racing like seven dwarfs.

I was nervous to a point of no return.
I knew I could trust him, so I let him...
take his turn.
He approached me, I saw his Adams apple drop
as he swallowed.
"I love you and I'll take care of you like
no tomorrow"
I let his words bounce off my ear drums
and create melodies in my head...
like a snare drum.
My panties were wet
water gun status.
I clenched my teeth cause I was
drowning in this madness.

He was a nice person, handsome was his name.
I knew it'd be a matter of time before I...
played him at his own game.
God didn't understand these urges.
My body was calling, and I needed some service.
So his phone rang ...he answered,
and it made me feel worthless.
-"She's ready, let's get it crackin."
I finally got a chance to make love,
so I didn't ask no questions.

Another guy entered the room...
said he was going to record.
-"Ay if you get tired of watching,
just hop on aboard."
Forcing my legs apart like a tool...
He drilled my sweet kitty like,
a word unknown_____
We were making love, but it felt so wrong!
"My sweet virgin," as he dripped sweat on my face.
I couldn't move anymore, my soul was constrained.

When we were done I didn't
know what to do.
He was my first love
and he was courteous too...

I said goodnight to him as he left
-and farewell to ms. virginity too...

Death by Mic

Before I woke up to the sweet sound of such bass and lyrics

It felt like my ears were feasting upon sweet potatoes and cornbread

And every sound bite was filled with wonderful pleasures

I couldn't imagine my taste buds

if the melodies couldn't dissolve into the pits of my heart

but I was very ill

Things became stuck in my esophagus

The newer generations made me wonder what planet this was

The words no longer matched the videos

The microphones became poisoned and the media

Replicated the bacteria

I do not honor this type of thesis

Feces grow from ignorant and greedy mindsets

Living like life is timeless

When in the real time is time set

And they only reproduce the sinful mother goose

Until it destroys the youth and nobody cares for truth

But when it spits back in your face, the diseases of the cactus

Be aware of such thorns, ready to obliterate all access

ENDLESS LOVE

ENDLESS LOVE? How can I speak of such?

When one doesn't cherish what he has?

Though I love so deep, and I love faithfully...

How can you taste me, when your love is tainted?

I don't require you to be a saint for me...

I know we all have flaws...

But I do require fulltime care

Just because I work for love.

I work for love because I believe

that believing in love will place me

in a reality that saves me...

And cherishes me for eternity.

Censored

The chronicles of a woman scorned

By nightmares or fallen dreams

Like stitches of an unborn wound

Ready to mount horrible terrors on the temple

        Beneath the benedictions of the crimson

        How can she not stomach the cleansing -

        Of much needed propaganda?

                Yet one cannot live by glory

            If they only devour thy opportunities

                With no one following

                But negative inaugurations

She kicks at the air like pillow soft tears

And she swallows all her pride in exchange

For mercy

        Her nervousness prowls

        Like déjà vu

        The stimulation is stone dead

        Concentration difficult

                He reaches out to her

                She grabs the Messiah

Her faith begins to walk literally

As it exits her body and into the mist

Tell the mainstream not to censor this

Nickelodeon

Used to be my favorite
First thing in the morning
With a fresh bowl of cereal
Fruity Pebbles, Fruit Loops, Captain Crunch, the regular

But what's worse now?
Adult swim
Or the backwards sentences?

By custom it submits immobility
Stuck in the dry cuts of jibberish
Consider bitter predicaments
With tons of hidden guerilla warfare

But most of us
Would rather just not know
Trust me,
I loved Rugrats, Face, and Bear in the Big Blue House

Either then
I felt more secure
Or I was simply a child in the makeup of the world

Back when it felt good to pretend
But then pretending became sickly
So it no longer stood a chance
in misery

And back when
Dreams actually mattered
But now it seems the matter depends on the dream

Cause if it don't fit BBB's standards
Then it really don't mean a thing

Back then, when Nickelodeon was my friend
Or was it all just pretend?

A Dime for a Quarter

Trading me

Is like replacing a quarter with a dime piece

Fifteen cents behind me

Dignity opposing honesty

Like choosing a Honda over a Lexus

No air condition or side view mirrors

The money to purchase it but just too cheap

To know the

Difference

Like knowing the purpose in deliverance

But taking the back end

Mimi ninaitwa ni...

Na wewe je?

Mimi ninapendo sana

But that's just my own wrong doing

Should've stopped when I realized

I wasn't priority

Inferior

Minority

SIMPLE

To be honest,

I should use the American flag to wipe away all the

tears of the souls that cry

when the "WHO AM I"

is questioned, constrained, blamed, raped, misled, dead, and abused.

These choices we choose,

the flag should be black and blue,

for every bruise, and for all the lying news.

History is fiction

Short and simple

Before You

They would negotiate our friendships silently

Like an incubator on death row

Too loyal again

This time it's a felony

I should be ashamed of myself for such

There was never a reason to stay beside any of you

I always seemed to do the most

Mirror mirror, I'm a joke

Years never accounted for quality magnificence

It's like they never even existed

Must be some type of coincidence

But THANK GOD for all of you

I regret no bits of it

Now I am whole

The sister my mother never had

I see your life sparkle in my eyes

The quality of sisterhood, no imitation can reproduce

The originals

A flower in the sun

You've grown right through me

Between the breaks in the pages

I saw my opportunities

And to become so exquisite

In combination with your reflection

In many ways it was scary

Other times, it was perfection

The kind that you dream about

But you wake up to a nightmare

A black hole

The sudden whisper of death

I can't see my air -

Without you being one of my lungs

Couldn't see no pair without Twin City building strong

Because before you

I was just a diamond in the dirt...

Nowadays I know friendship

You remind me

Of what I'm worth

Sour Apple Face

Dingy clothing and breath full of piped smoke
Good name brand, but educationally stripped
You like a lady in the streets, but a freak in the king
Well don't expect to break my castle with no type of
ring

Look at me now, you see my sour?

My teacher told me I would never amount to
anything
So while she is teaching children who are flunking
I am graduating college with distinction
Leading communities with compassion
Being a black poet of history
Now let's pause and solve this mystery
Who's watching who?
They'd rather watch me excel than to witness you
lose
But this is just all my own bird's eye
The haters be creeping, but I bet you know why
So I never allow my faith to be denied
Cause I do it by faith, and never by sight
Deceit is birthed from the eyes…
Whispers from all walks of life…
So who told you how to judge me?
That type of "just" isn't right

Look at me now, you see my apple?

I am not Brazilian
I do not speak in tongues

Not a red bone
But I respect where I'm from
Brown skin beauty, angelic smile
Anything less is plain denial
This is not boasting, I count my blessings

Look at me now, you see my face?

Pizza Hut

Chi City
The pizza hut literally
Not the company
I' ve experienced reality first hand
No offense
That deep dish drug that gives you munchies all
over again
Pizza kingdom, New York can' t hold even half of it
That give it to me daily, like some soul food & kool-
aid
That downtown beauty, Garrets popcorn and that
sugar baby

I assure you
If you' ve never laid your hands upon that Windy
City crust
Life has lied to you
If you' re satisfied with alternatives, ultimatums,
and the re-do' s
Several will try to imitate
But let' s get one thing clear
Taste of Chicago will get you wet enough, if your
pockets lean

Then add it up

That ooo weee ooo weee

Can' t get rid of it

Even thin crust takes my innocence

Sometimes I just can' t handle it

But I promise I always benefit

It impregnates me – fornication

I' m always bloated

Head over hills⋯

Boy oh boy, sweet Chicago meals

A Dozen Puzzles

Loving me must be like a dozen puzzles
Every time I pursue a mission
Impossible
The theory never works out and the hypothesis is proven
WRONG
I try to situate myself and be patient cause God said good
things come
When you wait...
Even when I fall and I pray
I still only find... empty boxes
Maybe it's no one's fault but my own
Perhaps I'm too strong and others can't take me head on
I apologize for my ignorance of not knowing how to be
So simple
My mind is too influential and my heart is original

If I make pretend, you'd call me phony'
When I keep it real, I'm too complex
Should I become phon-plex?
No sarcasm intended
It's like I put in one hundred and receive
Twenty five...cents
Or I fall in love
And you take a sky dive...

Or maybe I'm not attracting the correct consumers
What is it that I lack -
That you NEED?
What is it that I don't give -
But you feed?
What is it that I just can't do?
Must I bend my knees and wear a leash for you?

Take me as I am
Mirror to mirror
And if you can't see a clear picture
Then the dollar store sells Windex for a buck
And you're just out of luck to think I'm willing to suck

The life out of myself
Just so you can get a nut

Cold cuts...
Maybe me and all my pieces are too much
Or maybe you just bad at adding up to your own standards
Question & Answers

A dozen of you
But only one me

White

Snowflakes

Cocaine

White rain

Paper

Walls

White pain

People

Cars

White change

Gold

Souls

Kibbles & Bits

Silence

Come full equipped

No hide and seek please

Urgent

Breathe

Swallow

Battle field

Bow and arrows

Like gunplay

Frisky

Royal rumble

Hands in the air

No foul

Play

Fair

Soak it up

Body rock

Every

Little

Bit

Yum Yum Yum

Any refills?

L.O.V.E (Live Outside Vulgar Entities)

For a second I thought

There was chance inside of a failure

And that the turbulence of a nigga

Could transition into a field of

-Candy rain and loose leaf pain

-Physically free and mentally maintained

But in between heart and ache

I was kidnapped

Somebody told the police I was dead

And that was that

Nobody ever looked for me

Not even a flimsy cold case

I was lost in the zone

My spirit had been raped

And I chased the same dream

Several times

I got nine lives

And I lost all mine

Due to the sick and selfish

Of the sick and helpless

I couldn't even get fed

If I was eating breast milk

I was dying systematically

L.O.V.E was attacking me and it

Had the audacity

To rope, chain, and shackle me.

A prisoner in my own hope

I was hoping it was a joke until I choked

On the filthiness of emptiness

And when I begged for my life

I was stabbed with contempt

Left to bleed like rainfalls

And tornados grew inside of me

Knocking my joints out

Nobody ever looked for me

Not even a flimsy cold case

I was lost in the zone

My spirit had been raped

Dosage 9: A Step Ahead

209

Water Lilies

Don't you wish you could levitate away from the
destruction?

Into the skies like galaxies – one world – one mission

Or walk through walls to stop tragedy from releasing its pores of evil

Laughing in the face of the hypocrites

Don't you wish you could walk on water?

Save the titanic, drowning babies, homicide victims

Execute victory

What if we were water lilies?

Beautiful all the time, without error

Capturing life's purpose with the glimmer of your petals

Reproduction

Mama,

I know you acknowledge my presence as I

Use my feet to kick at your belly button and get your attention   just to let you know

I'm listening

I can tell that you've been through a struggle by the way your voice vibrates

When you speak

And by the roughness of your heartbeat when you cry into your pillow at night

I love you

Even when the world seems void

And I'm sorry in advance for the pains that I may cause you during labor

And for my terrible twos, my teen years, college loans, and more

I won't let you down

You've been through too much already

Good things will come to you

I just wish that I could say it personally myself

Maybe I'll babble to your heart

Mother and child love letter

And when finally I am born

I'll show you I was worth it

And when life plants me seeds – I'll grace you with its mercy

Spiral Staircases

It's funny how the world goes
Upside down

My angel's angel doesn't even want to be near
me
I cry tears of frost bitten fantasies

My brain cells have gone mindless
Curious George
Elliptical transactions

I surrender
I will
I must

This repetition is driving me up the wall
And my skin crawls like a reverse Niagara Falls
Scratch and sniff

I never win these games
Stereotype

Machine washable
Like I'm materialistic

Cannibal has it
Vegetarian mindset

Four leaf clover
Not erasing the time yet

They come in doubles
Violence lives outdoors

There's a pitch fork
And I'd rather be the pork

214

The destination doesn't stop here

In fact, it never does

And when they ask who am I…

Tell them I never was

Different Window View

Escape.Exit.Leave.Remove.Transform.Evolve.Go.Take.Break.Push.Away.Isolate

That	Read
Route	Between
Is	All
Much	The
Easier	Lines

Fail.fall.lose.break.hate.revenge.evil.sin.pretend.lie.cheat.defeat.war.pride.insult

Can	Read
You	It
See	Until
It	You
Now?	Do

Wicked.envy.cruelty.jealousy.dishonest.promise.unjust.deceive.mislead.hyprocrisy

What if this was my view of you?

216

Toy Story

The child awakens

It finds pleasure in its circumstances

Anytime things become broken - they are easily replaced

Smiles are fabricated

Everything is painted accordingly

He picks up his soldiers

She plays in her doll house

Everything is happy

Emotions don't exist now

Just a world full of satisfaction

Warranties guaranteed

They could see no evil

For plastic really doesn't breathe

It just is

And it felt so good

No one could stop the greatness

No dreams deferred

But sometimes things just never occur

Man,

What I would give

To have a toy's story

A MOTHER'S SPINE

Holds sickness at high risk when her child is filled with
coughs and fevers
And will go to the extremes to see that everything is
eventually healed
Even if it means she gets ill helping you
She defers her own dreams
Just to ensure you see yours
She understands your immaturity
But acknowledges your worth
Knowing that every strong will
Takes plenty of time to grow
Its life
And she is patient during the worst
When you panic at life's tiniest upsets
She smiles to remind you that you're simply
Being too hard on yourself
And encourages you NOT to quit…
But to do better next time
Her spine does not break when your heart shuts down
Her hand does not close
When your eyes are in denial
There is no better place than the love a mother owns
Anything less than the above -
Is a girl still in school
And that goes far beyond a university's curriculum
A mother's chores are learned
But her heart is already present
To give more than to receive
To nurture and replenish

218
These things in life are free
Even when its counterparts are expensive
There is no substitute

Biological or not
A mother is not defined by who can open her legs to receive
But is defined by the quality and wisdom she leaves unto her
seeds

Book Bag

Would you like to know what I carry on my back?

1 day of harassment

16 years of education and counting

Several lost "friends" and a few additions

1 heartbreak perhaps

2 grandmothers gone – one still alive but as heartless as a thorn

The other was my everything, but I must not mourn forever

1 amazing mother

1 lost, ignorant father

3 siblings

1 super best friend

1 amazing crew – you know who you are

1 family

1 God

1 life

22 years and I've fallen quite a bit, but I'm still standing

Tomorrow is not promised, so before my spine caves in

Thanks for helping me sort out my book bag

Corinthians

There is only one way to know

Truth

Open up and read

Stop guessing

Making assumptions

Lying

And misleading

Verse thirteen

I guarantee you it's a sure thing

In every single version

Love is etc

Make it known through Christ

The difference between pretending and knowing

Love Notes Invisible

I see them

The words

They tickle my eyes like feather weights

I hear them

The sounds

They vibrate my ears like blind dates

I can't seem to feel them though

That's one problem I can't seem to solve

"I Love You"

Never reached my mind at all

My heart has considered it

But my mind tells me it's not legit

Darn you sentences

Why must you be so empty?

Stepping Out

I'm leaving for good

Walking out on the world

Today, present time

I have zero tolerance for hatred

For it is disrespectful to my purpose

I want no part of it

I don't believe in it

I do not recommend it

I don't understand it

In fact, I don't want to

It is endless here

So without it I will proceed

It's just not for me

Unreal Reality

I never thought it would be this hard

The words "good bye"

It demolishes me like project buildings

Except for all the roaches and rats

Its pain, hunger, and blood shed tears

I tried sleeping on it

Only to find sleepless nights and degrading dreams

I tried counting on it

Only to find blank numbers

I tried avoiding it

Just to find repetitive issues

I tried to replace it

But found myself drowning in tear filled tissues

I guess I miss you

I never saw it coming

The moment of departure

I got used to being sick with you beside me...

I adapted to your lifestyle – I tolerated it

Now I must learn to live life again on my own

Goodbye Cancer

Revulsion

When you cough and don't cover your mouth

       Chew with your mouth open
       Pass gas, its natural – but say EXCUSE ME

       Involve me in he say/she say

       Don't take care of your children

Disrespect the elderly

       Take what's not your own

Lie on me

Volunteer to be stupid
    Don't moist your lips when you expect a kiss – SIKE

       Breath smells like golden days

                       AIDS

Animal cruelty
       Rape and harassment

                Domestic Violence

No standards

       Racism

              Sexism

Duplicate people

Insects & reptiles

Pedophiles

Dosage 10: Forever Like Destiny

Just a Mattress

Soft and pleasant as I rest my skull on the soft utters beneath me;

      teething on energy lost.

Buried upon the quilt are the sheets

      holding my figure in place as I rest.

My black outline sinks into the shadows   in

memory of my loving grandma.

When revealed, one see's the stains;   once

touched by her shaking hands-

wondering what caused her to spill   such

liquids on an unknown demand.

So even when I dress the bed,   I

picture me by her organs as I settle.

For this blessing once was hers;

      something to sooth her mind with.

Laying upon her presence even if   she

is far beyond the sky's eyes.

I lay in memories of such disguise   by

no surprise, I close my blinds.

For this is not just a mattress,   I feel

her touch me with security-

wrapping me with wisdom and

loving me with opportunity.

One day this mattress will distort, and when it does I will call it

art!

Fly To You

I feel you as the hairs on my back rise when you stand
behind me

When you shelter me when danger is near, I know your
there too

I'd like to speak to you sometimes
Just because I listen when you whisper to my heart

You dare me to do better

But sometimes I don't know where to start
It's hard out here
But I assume you're acquainted with the hands on the clock

I think you're amazing
Nothings different from when you were actually here
Except your warm hugs and kisses

But we still communicate
And that's all I ask for
That you never leave me in the spiritual form

Thank you
For always taking the time to visit me
And to ensure my heart stays in one piece

I am who I am partly because of you
Nowadays I see you in my mother's face
And just in case you were wondering
I'd prefer no other to take your place

You always do the most for me
Do tell God I said, I'm grateful

The best part about this is
I shine due to your halo...

I just wish that I could fly to you instead of you to me
So we could just catch up on things
I hope you're proud of me

Animalistic

The ego

Sometimes the enemy

How dare it stare me in the face with danger awaiting?

She stares back with aggressive pupils

I dare not look at times

But I always feel challenged

Her bark swallows my meow

And my chirp is consumed by her howl

I still don't back down

Time is going backwards now

I attend the battle field

Head on

But when I was ready to confront her

She was gone

Until next time

I had won

Cajun Love

I need to be able to taste it
The chemistry between us
I need you in my atmosphere like
Outer space need Venus

Fulfill me
You need it as much as I do

Mentally stimulate my taste buds
And play with my dignity
Transform my expectations
And teach me with sincerity

When were spiced up
No one can do it better
Don't need no herbal tea
We can simply cure each other

Too Deep to Heal

Looking into your eyes I find myself the victim of
gunshot wounds

Instant kill at point blank range

How I survived?

I prayed

The moment I decided to program my life based on
your standards

I lost my own quality

Downgraded just for an orgasm

And all you did was decorate the hurtful truth

But I knew it was a lie from how it killed my roots

I recognized the disguise from a mile away

And since I witnessed every fall

I guess I died that day

No trace of homicide left behind

You were never satisfied

I was left denied

And while I sit and rematch the pieces of my spine

I'd love to tell you how you genuinely

Blow my mind

It can't heal this time

Like Water

Emerged in the depths of tranquility

Thinking of reasons to dispose all quarts of hostility

A hazard

Justified by methods unknown

The thoughts on the wall fall frequent

To each its own

When it's time to gasp for air

You inhale deeper

The steeper the pain

The better the climb

And if one thing is in relation to the next

Then life is just a bomb

And stress is not a threat

A courageous mind would run

Forest green

And anything below is just a world

Unseen

Concrete Flames

I seen it
With my own eyes
It came in pure day light
Not at night
It has been present for centuries
I am not the first

Be alert
What you don't know will kill you
Your last worry might be
Your first nightmare

Open 24/7

It's not like the candy store where you love every piece of candy
your mouth can hold

Nor is it like your favorite shopping outlet

Where you get off by the latest fashion trends

Let's become acquainted with the term "over-rated"

So you can keep it moving

And miss out on the pregnancy, STD 's, and disappointments

Maybe you won't have to consider an abortion

Or maybe you're so star struck that you do the exact opposite

Just know that if your legs rotate like analog clocks

A virus will infect the entire darn hard drive

And who knows what that'll lead to

All types of changes, neglect, and needles

Is it really worth it?

Just to defeat the purpose?

To rush into the store -

And refund your virgin?

Tiger Breath

Isolation

Punctuation

Hard core

Masculinity

Edgy

Just a boy

Masturbate

The

Ignorant Mindset

Deep

Breath

Oasis

Just Like Puberty

Sensitive and senseless

Vulnerable to the world

In training

Growth by expectations

Cloudy minded

With a chance of sunshine

Sound familiar?

This is not the description of a child

This is the blank blank blank

That you have chosen not to love

A MOTHER'S DAY

I can assure you that you mean the most,

and to deny that truth would be for me to boast.

And I'd never take all the credit for this woman I've become.

Because through you I have swallowed a strong willed tongue.

Because of you, I have found a me.

My soul provides tears of peace, knowing that you made time to nurture me.

Twenty two years later, I still feel the same.

And I thank God that he placed me inside the womb of a queen.

I Love You Mommy,

You're only

Destined by Quality

He doesn't seem to know his purpose
Everything is detrimental
The worst has become his mindset
Leaving improvement on a noose
He is zealous to detach himself
With no assembly line instructions on how to put
him back together
Not even a blue print to the heart
He forecloses it
The vacancy of emotions has forced her to notice this
Calling...

She cannot reach him from the outer shell
If she should speak
She is cursed by the scorned ticking bomb
Jeopardizing her own organ to see that
His beats too
Two people
One in a hole
The other who seeks to
Relinquish the hunger he eats through – just to
prove that she is worthy
And that the truth is bound to bleed blue
When the only thing holding a bond is just you
And the mirror clowns laugh when they see
A failed pair

But she dares to quit so easily
Or she will never know...
Was it worth it to hold on
Or to simply let it go...

He has a place in her heart – even when it has
shattered stained glass style
But she has known better – to leave the past in the
past NOW
And nothing is guaranteed – happiness is a virtue

Yet contempt in your heart
Will abolish those who love you

Dosage 11: Growth

He Saw the BEST in Me

Manipulated
secretly hated
Unappreciated

Through burning eyes I have issued myself an identity that no one can
take from me
From the flow of my blood through the cells in my skin, from the
heart and my oxygen
From my lost to my wins and my circles and spins I have prospered
and I have remained non-dizzy
I have fallen, I have crashed, I have given up, I have laughed

With this humble soul I have broken through the temptations of hell
I have envisioned myself in life to excel, prevail
You see God is my official, from Him I learn, to Him I turn
I am a leader in His kingdom, not just a leader at my university
No hater, no faker, no traitor will hurt me
God gave me the courage and I told Him I will stand
I will stand even when they see the worst in me
Every flaw or imperfection, your denial, your rejection
I am not to be confused, I am not to be misused
I am not to be destroyed, or even misconstrued

I am God's poet and I'll die knowing this
When it is time for me to take my place and my soul excels to
a better place, I owe my highest thanks to the one who takes...

My pain away when I am in a hole in the ground, He opens my mouth
and feeds me nouns
Pulled me from the rib of man and gave me this plan and said to
follow Him

He dries my tears when they fall and He guides me when wrong
Shapes me, molds me, and has faith in me even when I have none in I

In I is where He invests his time and I'd be too blind if I denied
I claim not to be great, but I claim this faith. Kirk said I sing because
I'm happy, Sapp said I never would have made it. Lady agrees with
them both, but I say that even when I'm crawling and I force myself in
this mindset of disability - when in reality God is where I need to
invest my rationality, the battle is not always for me to fight, and God
is my savior and God has the light. I have fallen in the footsteps of a
Man who loves me, he loves me genuinely, not for what I posses
under my skirt, and not for a tool. This love is like no other love, I
have found this man to be too good to be true, but little did I know
that He is the reason why...

I have overcome so many obstacles. I have fallen and I have crawled.
I have searched and I have jumped. I have bled and I have been lost.
But when He grabbed my hand and chose to stand by me forever, He
looked me in the soul and breathed He'd never leave me ever.

Every bone in my body to the muscle that surrounds it, thank you God
for giving me such talents. For the love that I have and the things that
I've lost. Because loss doesn't always mean that you are in a losing
position. Sometimes it's a sign for you to walk away from submission.
It is our pride that kills us and it is our God that keeps us. It is our
selfishness that strips us of the full picture and it is our ignorance that
breaks us.

Ladies and gentlemen wake up,
life is so much more than the clubs, the hoes, the foes, the cash
the cars, the drugs, the violence, the infidelity, and I could go on and
on if I had more time, but time is not promised so I'm taking this time
to share my knowledge. I'll give for you if you give for me. One soul,
two minds, more dignity. I am not perfect, but I have a vision and God
saw it. I will pursue this vision because this is my mission. My life is
the experiment and I will find the cure. God is my lens and I will look
right through Him. In Him I will find my purpose and in Him I will find
the reason. In Him I will rid any bypassing demon.
In Him I will.....as He has chosen me....

I am so successful today...
Because He saw the BEST in me...

251

AND THERE WAS YOU

Coming into context with the battle scars
I have obtained...
Not by choice but by force because I was a
character to another's game.
If you don't understand what my heart is speaking
let me be more direct.
I'm a survivor of past relationships, the drama, neglect...
EX, AFTER EX...
Yes, I shout in rejoice because God has a plan.
I shall not despise the last guy that had me in his hand.
And I refused to let a past fling ruin a designed destiny.
Battle scars and broken hearts, a part of my symmetry.

How dare you tell me "to stop writing for you."
satan must have knocked all of your loose screws...loose.
To give up my heaven sent for something so ungrateful,
Let me give you a tea spoon, so you can taste my ego.
Yet, I pray for your happiness and not only you...
The one before you pressured me for sex like I was a prostitute.
At my WORST, I kept it, so what makes you think you could
tempt me at my BEST? You love me? Sure you do...or do you
love the thought of what's in between...
my legs?

Yet, I still pray for them. And no regrets lay upon my pillow
As I have grown because of them.
And then..
AND THEN,..THERE WAS YOU.
Who?
I never imagined my heart to intertwine
so blind yet right in front of me, tasty...wine.
A God fearing, but God loving man, so gentle...a gentleman &
handsome.
I breathe you from within. Your smile so enlightening
so bright...that it is frightening, to envision you on my lips

like a tornado on a bright day.
Making love through chemistry and building bonds of intimacy,
not through sexually explicit, but mentally gifted.
Heavenly lifted, I accepted you...
You and I and it feels so right.
This is new to me, never dated one like you...
So very patient...
Pure like me, how could this be?
That WE need meet?
I never thought it'd be YOU...
Combine with me.

So as always I stand hopeful,
and I choose, to stand by you…
You won't need no one else...no celeb fantasy idol.
Just me, and I ...you.
I'll carry you through; I'm down for you black and white
No plain residue.
Believe me, that you...
Can trust in me to…Give you all you need...
Just me and you

The haters can hate, but we shall prosper
Beneath all the pain,
You've earned my honor.
My eyes are wide open and I
won't look for them...in you.
Ahead is our future...because...

There was you…

If oxygen were painted black and eyes were able to see it move like
sickness in the veins of a survivor-
like a bird with no beak, I see you stare at me like prey.
Yet you don't want to feast upon my delicate compounds-
you'd rather heal my wounds and seal any entrance that may be
subject as a target, cold blooded and hardened, dangerous: Larceny
For some have taken what has not been their own
and being vulnerable is a sickness in its own.

How I would love to be your centerpiece-
bonded by immunity and love beyond chemistry.
Where I can taste the hunger on your lips and digest the curiosity of
your body-
to unfold to you like a flower and feed to you as to devour.
Cowards copy and paste your image to disguise and hide their filth,
like a silver spoon
burdened by spoiled milk.
The sour taste on the tongue like residue when it's speaking-
but the truth comes out eventually, hypothetically thinking.

Centerpiece

Allow me to release my womb to you as to paint a master image
But if my heart isn't good enough, I shall damn this whole sentence.
Forbidden like the apple from Adam's mouth, how sinful you are to
degrade my health.

Though out of fear I hide from you like a naked sheep
and I curl into fetal like an aborted seed.
Ready to bleed only because I expect the worse-
constrained mentally by intellectual whips and chains

Not knowing how to let go of such flesh eating pains.
As I scratch this itch that has been embedded into my spirit-
I know now that I can deal because I feel it in my interest.
My spine has been curved for too long, been breaking my back for the
ignorant- with no love in return.
I want to feel the skins of reality and walk past death,
on my way to actuality. Protect me as I get off my knees and stand,
as I conquer this voice that was bred deep inside of me like a plague,
So when I walk with my voice no longer strained-
Define me as your centerpiece, a star beyond a gaze.

Mountains Fall

Mountains fall

Like dominoes

It's just hard for us to see them

They crawl and they walk

It's just hard for us to be them

They cry and they laugh

It's just hard for us to read them

They win and they lose

It's just hard for us to appreciate them

Despite all the things that mountains might do

They still stand tall...

Unlike me and you

Cubic Squares

With every part of me

All of the heart of me

In the dark of me

And the scarred of me

Like a box of me

Milky chocolate me

I give you all of me

The cubic squares of me

Pencils, Erasers, & Paper

One thing

In

Common

The history

Of

Poetry

The soul

Of

Unique minds

The struggles

Of

Slavery

The master

Of

258

Arts

The ace of spades

And hearts of hearts

With One Touch

It could be here today

Gone

Tomorrow

Built on love

Or pints of

Sorrow

Hard right now

And

Brighter later

Poor to you

But

Death to another

With one touch

You can be corrected

So shut your mouth

COUNT THE BLESSINGS

Size Matters

I mean doesn't it matter to you?

I love how it stimulates me

Without the use of a rubber

It's incredible

It took me a while to grow into it

I like to challenge it

Some multiplication or moody music

Nowadays it feels heaven sent

I'm in love with this head game

The wonderful mind of a woman

Something that can never be replaced

Get your act together

This isn't that!

While you're worried about someone's Jimmy

I'm convinced I'm better than that...

Taking Me Back

Ready to make sense of everything I've been
lacking
Spent too much time on yesterday and too less
time
On now
You don't deserve to interrupt my flow of existence
Yes, I am judging you!
Because the last time I checked, you proved me
right
I no longer care for you in the way I once did
You're not a slob, nor a pig, you're just worthless
A human
Seeking to suck the life out of the willing
Ready to kill without healing
And able to lie with no feeling
But my life is no longer parallel to your acute
stupidity
I'm dealing with me now
And this is just so bitter free

I need to thank you, literally
For everything you did for me
I freaking love you mirror!
You've been the best part of me

Did you really think that I was speaking such truth
of you?
You couldn't fit that description if I paid you to
I'm taking me back

I deserve that much
I'll admit it
You're worth it
A bag of chips and some nuts
Oh boy — I crack myself up
But the joke is over now
That's enough

I'm taking me back

IF IT WERE ME

If it were me, I'd drop dead at the beauty of your fragrance,
As I penetrate your mind just so it can cum
Run-on like a sentence, you have my permission
Lift every voice and sing to my attention
I need to visualize your flesh
Just so I can memorize your skeleton
And when I have it perfect
I shall never let the pain turn wrong
Or let the tongue of misery regurgitate you
I would save you, so you can be introduced to
The courteous...
Not the verb-less stress of a nest that has transpired
While under pressure, which would
Break me...to see
You
Vulnerable
Like a stone in the air coming down in a pool
Helpless to float
Sunken like a titanic
But never had that chance, never granted satisfaction!

If it were me, I'd take in the smoke of cigarettes
And hold it all inside my lungs, along with the oil spills,
I'd drink the dirty waters and I'd swallow all the waste
If I internally bleed to death, I'd be the cure
To pollution
And birds can fly and fish could swim
In pure resolution

If it were me, I'd take justice and flush it down
the toilet,
and take a suction tube while it's in breech position
and abort it
I'd cut off its umbilical cord so those who have been victims
Fall right out

Then recycle its whole demeanor
And spit the bible right out.
Since God is King of the light house
Then its justice He turn the lights out.

Into Me

She looked me in the eyes
I could tell she was interested
Her body language seemed to be hesitant but her
heart
Was more eager
I tried to avoid the situation
But she spoke first
From that moment on
I knew I had found my first

She was beautiful intellectually
And I noticed she had a story to tell
I listened
Her history smelt pleasing
And I needed to take a sip of it

She was kind, but aggressive
Stubborn in all the right places
The voice of a Queen and the heart of the same

I never met anyone quite like her
I closed the bathroom mirror
I wonder who wants to wife her?

Dosage 12: Deciphered

Ameri-Kill

America,
Embedded with hidden meanings that are-
left un-deciphered at all angles.
Robbing the baby from its cradle-
with whispers no longer silent.

America,
We are not blind, yet most of us roll up our tongues-
like a red carpet, refusing to speak out and be voiced
by choice.
For America has created a 360 degree battle field.
Freedom will never exist, even embryos are-
born into this plan of shit.

How careless America,
when in fact it is Ameri-Kill.
Abortions, racism, sexism, age-ism
If I continue naming all of the issues
God will paralyze my hand-
because by the time this world sees true peace
it must be re-created again.

America, with your lies.
This hierarchy of evil-
and we the people hypnotized by images
underneath us.
Breathing air that internally murders.
Digesting the blood our ancestors
died to fight against.
We recreate the violence-
eager to kneel in silence.

America,
Even if portrayed on TV-
a culture of broken promises, fame is all mischief

268

And there is no such thing as turning the other cheek.
Cause as soon as you do right
society says you just wrong-
and by the end of the ceremony
America buries you in a tomb.

Those who strive to create change
are ignored out of fear.
But even if they don't like it,
I speak, PRESENT, I'm here.

America,
How sinful to sketch this world as a symbol
of death before time-
I pledge allegiance to my pencil.

FALLING

When I *ran* to his arms

       No one

Was there

To embrace me

Vacancy

Without Light

Transitions of negativity

The illusion of love's asset

We are nothing but a wanna-be

Without the investment

Some call them fathers

But him

I call sorry

Some hate the images

I forgive the fallen

Becoming a woman

WHITE RAIN

You remind me of this unicorn that lay its head upon the fallen
clouds
and just because it wanted to engage in pillow talk
I went to sleep
Just to dream
I swam through your words as I ate every syllable
swallowing your underlined love song
Regurgitating the musical notes that I can't seem to
put into words of my own

And when I wake up
I can't seem to understand why
the king of hearts only sent me
aces and spades
Why the rain wasn't clear
when the clouds fell that day
I became lost in the dream and your unicorn came to me
It looked me in the eyes and it
cried to me
How beautiful it was
it reminded me of you
The tears of the pony were white
and it rained on me like destiny

Damned Photo

I took a photo of the psychic in front of me
Partially
Because I wanted a savored moment of my life
On her tongue
As her thoughts create drums
Inside of her own

In the photo, I saw it
My future was liquidation
The cup right in front of her –
My entire simulation
And she drank it –
I watched her
Through this photo

I saw my faith floating on the walls
And my curiosity on her face
I captured my passion in her eyes-
She must've felt what I –
ATE

But that was before I –
Burned it
The whole damn image
Her crystal ball was no more
Than the tear drop that masturbated my face
I didn't want things so obvious!
Ambiguity creates STANDARDS

Who said I believe in psychics?
When mankind can't even answer…
What is the difference between art and war?
A heart of slots –
Is a world of infinite inserts

So what do I need with –
A PHOTO?
When the people will just Photoshop
And edit
My threshold…

ENTITLED

Because the truth is –

    the equity of my existence has *expired*.

        and whoever keeps
      drinking my vomit

I
s

j
u
s
t

a
s

r
u
i
n
e
d

a
s

I

a
m

Hypocrisy

I am just

As dumb

As you are

If you think the law is for us

And if

I'm wrong about you

The

Law

 Must be wrong

About me

Life

In between the pores of life

an ivory opportunity arrives

Sometimes…

We would rather live than die.

So much that love is a sickle celled disease –

and at ease, it takes over like diabetes.

Once in a lifetime, my time is precious -

to those who take their time

to give my time

a lesson.

Something that the trees cannot vaporize –

milk chocolate grounds and vanilla skies.

And my compounds decompose like –

memories that give birth

to a dream.

To play the game of life

before life destroys the seam…

LOVE WAS, AND THEN

Sporadically, I condition my intuition to agree
with my heart
Due to its continuous battles and distant laughter -
I cry tear drops of tar and concrete memories
and sometimes they rub off like rubbish into a sea

See
I had once opened up my heart like a hand shake
I would take people's hands and turn them into a creation
of what I thought love was
But when we spoke it into existence
it transformed into a bus
and hit me

Love lost me quickly
Ruined now
I no longer constitute the pure illusion
My skin has become skinless and my organs
suffocate voluntarily -
I'd rather break my own heart
than for someone to do it for me

My story
Climbs walls and enslaves messages you cannot understand
The moment you put your eye on it
A crow will cast from hell
And we will watch it together
as it appears to fly away
But the quality of a dying dream
rejuvenates one's faith

That's what it seems like
Demons laugh at my pair
They come in the form of people
and try to emasculate my gains.

And once again
I try to condition my mind to agree
so that I never say that I didn t
give the other half of me
a chance to be free

Free to trust
lust
give up
praise
and discuss

Free to forgive
re-live
burn energy
and rust

Though I know
I have been enslaving myself
Betrayal
Selfish of me to allow the her in me
to fail
And to allow the pretty ugly
to jeopardize the beauty
so that the beast can ejaculate
and give birth to a lie

Because the truth is
the equity of my existence has expired
and whoever keeps drinking my vomit
is just as ruined as I am

She who cries hymns
soils the book of righteousness
with uncertainty
Not for the word
but for those who read it undeservingly

I can never convince the evolved self
to submit to its vulnerability
And maybe that's what love is...
Acknowledging the WE
in me

MARCH ON: A GRANDMOTHER'S WISH

And He spoke into her lungs
as she spoke into my eyes.
She - a warrior
The backbone to a family's battlefield.
Breaking off a part of herself each time -
Just to watch us live.

A nest inside God's Kingdom
She freshened me with nourishment.
My siblings and my cousins
A product of Thee Heaven Sent

Today, I acknowledge her date of birth
just because I know...
A woman's worth.

If there is anything left inside of me -
to inhale the memories vibrantly,
I'd digest every moment silently -
just so she can be the CRY in me.

For these are no longer lost pleas of sadness.
This is a warning...my ultra violet
My kisses and hugs
My grandma, I thank you
For watching this family
Our Holy Angel

Because above all of your flaws -
All I can see is perseverance
The struggles that you chewed
has now become our emancipation.

As much as we may not see it
or choose to ignore it.

The sky is NOT the limit
God is above it.

For when we surpass our expectations
we learn to expect a sure pass.
Yet, a house is not a home
until the FIRST becomes LAST.

My left brain misses your entire entity,
and my right brain is strong enough to know you still instill
in me -
the prerequisite I need,
to graduate my family.

Believe me Grandma, I heard you
and whenever you spoke...
I listened.
Just promise me one thing -
under any condition.

Let God know that I am trying and that -
I need you as my direction.
That I love you more than galaxies
as they nurture the solar system.

Promise me that you will march on
for there is no loss in a blessing.
So that we can follow your love steps,
and engage in the ultimate victory.

Regurgitate

My

Heart

I. No Air

I touched my abdomen with the tip of my finger
Breathing was different -
Oxygen was leaking
The mirror wasn't at distance
So I cater to it like cancer.
It peers into my flesh like x-ray vision
At this moment I am
Outside
Of
My own.
Touching the glass, I feel the outline –
Realizing that when I pull my hand back
It is moist
I could feel a part of me absent -
Darkness had survived and happiness had went to hell
Who do I trust now?
Who had walked inside of me -
And beat the shit out of my drum line?
An instrument tampered with one time too many
Still fighting against the genius – too smart for its own sense
Realistic versus emotion
Utopia against Dystopian
I turn away from the mirror and sit
A moment in time
Just me, my fingerprint
And the equator in my chest.

II. The Consumed

Nothing more to verbalize
Emotion is a death wish

It opens up your pores and kills you silently
You wear your heart on your sleeve
You commit suicide
I protect you from stupidity
You just settle for a lie
Cry –
Stained tears like red ink, no eraser
No pencil, no lead, black paper
Must be humble – Ask questions later
For who knows truth better than intuition?
He who follows the tongue
Will die by vengeance
But he who follows the mind –
Overcomes submission
Be sensitive to reality, and cautious to feeling
For the heart will not pump healthy without my stimulation
A heart without a brain -
Vegetable situation.

III. Abducted

I wake up on the floor – the mirror on top of me
Glass cut into my skin like a glass masterpiece
I felt nothing
My chest was thumping too fast
Migraine headache
You would think they both clashed.
No energy
I pick up a piece of the mirror and stare
The reflection was horrific –
My mind had consumed all the pain I once equipt-ed
It sunk its teeth into my purpose –
No longer a factor
Everything I ever was
Gone – Vanished
Can I please have me back…Mr. Damage?

Skeleton Go

She who
wishes to restore her imperfections,
seeks to do so with a –
ruined make up brush.
To blush -
away
frustrations engraved on tomorrow.
And so the heart beat breaks through-
creating incisions that no mascara
can hide.

Like two hundred and six – broken bones
One soul
NO LIFE

A fragile frame.   Yet
he praises the masturbated minds
One no photo can hold peacefully -   of the
sick greedy,
the decency alone in blind sight,
ignoring the thick layers-
she pretends to be.
immensely intruding on a sure thing.

He looks, eyes wide-
she seems to be inferior.
Justice by the bible,
but in it, he believes none.
The only one he gives thanks to
is the bastard in the mirror.
Had such a vision been any clearer,
he would die watching her breathe-
through his rib.
But with all the faces he may recycle and redistribute-
he may never know…
blood will never circulate…
and she can never grow…

So Much, So Little

I want to do so much

By saying so little

So I pick up my pencil and I

Write:

"The precautions of time do not exist where time is wasted

For patience is an option and those who greed will never taste it

And I too have fallen in the ocean of stress

And I too have eaten the fruit of disgust

With a thorn in my tongue

No gag effect

The world shall not *spun* in the present past of tense

In other words – go out and grab a planet

What's not in your control – is just an absence – vacant

Go see – it will rain but a rainbow will come

Cause to die without life is a life that's been gone"

 Signed:

Wake up call

From Purpose to Meaning

Like a seed beneath the roots of a fruit tree

I have watched you grow

Inside of me

How fruitful you are to replenish me every time

And how much I am not able to thank you

Because words, like love, isn't always enough

But even then I still love it

Like you

I do

Even when my actions don't bleed through -

Like Ink when it sings blues

And my arms paint images of armor –

With a blink

It's so easy for you

to say

That my mind is playing tricks

But like the number line, there is no amount of time

That can add up to the

undeniable

I have seen in you

And beyonce was wrong

1 + 1 doesn't equal 2

The solution is far more complicated than basic math

I'd break the ocean off

Just to see to it

You have half

With every laugh you infect me with

I'd give you a thousand suns

Just so you can say that love replenishes

To toast to the no return

Such a life of misfortune

The small things we don't know

Breathe a destiny of importance

To me you are for real

No distance can erase the face

The essence of being loved

The touch of grace

So when we salute to the growing pains

No addition can replace the lessons of change

For a dove will not fly without wings

and

a heart is just a shape

until it s filled with color schemes

So I ask you

Don't forget about those

The red

The blue

The gold

Trust me – I know

Even when you are afraid to admit it

Life is a train ride

You have been blessed with a ticket

I say to you

Beautiful

Black

Queen

You can succeed in anything

I simply

Serve as a crutch

So if ever it seems you can't

There is no thing as such

To see is to dream

To reach is to remember

To touch is to honor

But to live is to be thankful

I love you

And your color scheme

AMONGST US

There is a Queen amongst us, even unconscious maybe
For perhaps she doesn't even know it herself.
And to reaffirm that mannerism
the pigeons in her flock all hock the same
They call
She follows like an open hand
bread allows the hungry taste
of needed nourishment - at her distaste
Love
awaits
Eager on this day of great blessings
Bow your head dear Queen - give thanks to He
I honor Him, for allowing me
to feast upon your delicacy
with your abundance of intelligence
and your handful of hearts...
If Ace's spade kills the Joker
then dear Queen
The card I pulled is you
And even if you smile a little when you read this
My philosophy is you
If you love a little - give me
If you've lost a little - teach me
Cause a Queen like you must move
forward
Like the years placed blatantly inside of your timeline
But time lies
Because in my eyes -
Your beauty is infinity
Mentally, Spiritually, Emotionally....
Genuinely

Biography

Ambitious, loyal, faithful, compassionate, creative, and wise are only a few words to describe Author Nneka J. Howell. With this being her third published book at age twenty two, she has vowed to continue to lead others through the amazing world of creative writing. The Chicago born writer has recently graduated with distinction from the University of Illinois in Champaign-Urbana with a Bachelor of Arts in Communication. She plans to utilize her talents, skills, and abilities in graduate school within the upcoming years as she continues to stay active in the communities around her. For her, writing is not a hobby, but a lifestyle. There is nothing that feeds her soul like that of creative writing. In the future she plans to publish more work in order to reach individuals all over the world; helping them to acknowledge their own voices. Poetry may be where she emphasizes her passions; however, writing in general is something that she refuses to live without.

Hidden Candor: Deciphered by Voice is a compilation of various poems that have been written over the past few years. One can expect the silences to be broken and the truths to be revealed. If you are prepared for the unexpected, please enjoy the content in which Author Nneka J. Howell has bestowed upon you.

Also By the Author

A Poet's Heart

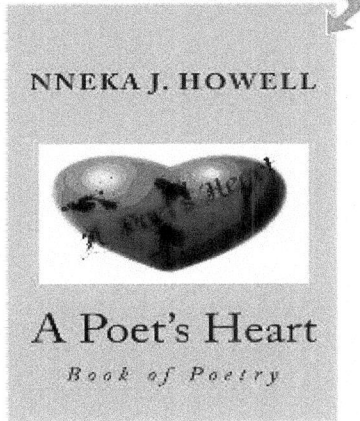

Real Women Get Their Hands Dirty

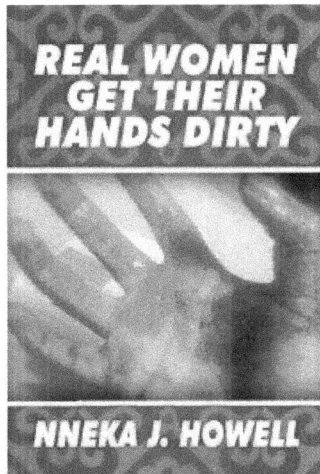

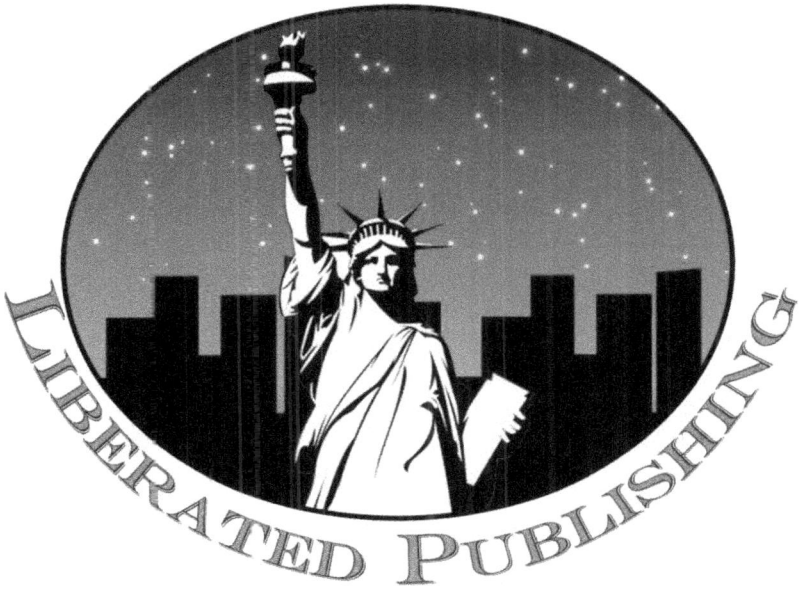

Liberated Publishing Inc.
1860 Wilma Rudolph Blvd
Clarksville, TN 37040
931-378-0500
info@liberatedpublishing.com
www.liberatedpublishing.com